For Faye.

JASON RIDDINGTON

LIFE, DEATH, TAI CHI AND ME
MY BRAIN INJURY JOURNEY

ILLUSTRATIONS BY GREGOR COPELAND

AUSTIN MACAULEY PUBLISHERS™

LONDON · CAMBRIDGE · NEW YORK · SHARJAH

A CIP catalogue record for this title is available from the British Library.

ISBN 9781035804658 (Paperback)
ISBN 9781035804665 (ePub e-book)

www.austinmacauley.com

First Published 2023
Austin Macauley Publishers Ltd®
1 Canada Square
Canary Wharf
London
E14 5AA

Table of Contents

Part 2

Foreword
by Alison Ryan

I first met Jason when he came to our service 3 months after a life-threatening subarachnoid haemorrhage and a month in hospital.

During our conversations, Jason was trying to make sense of what had happened to him. Who was the old me? And who is the new me? How do I make sense of, and process, what I saw as I came so close to dying? How do I live in this altered body and mind? What meaning do I make of all of this?

After our first session or two, I suggested Jason write about and 'journal' his experiences. This can often help people to process difficult memories. Jason found it helpful. He kept writing. Several weeks later, Jason realised he might have something to share about his experiences and reflections, which may help others. And here is the result! Like many of the people I have the privilege to work with, Jason's courage and determination humbles me.

What strikes me about this book is that it offers an honest and remarkable view into Jason's innermost world, in the aftermath of both a brain injury and a reminder of our mortality. The fact that Jason also happens to be a T'ai Chi expert adds another level to this account.

The relationship between T'ai Chi and healing of the mind, brain and body is well-known but little explored. Jason chronicles his use of T'ai Chi in the early days while still seriously unwell. The impact for him is remarkable. He continues his use of T'ai Chi as a central part of his recovery and healing, at the same time charting his spiritual journey. This book shares that exploration with the reader, through his story, his poetry and images.

This personal account will speak to people who have experienced brain injury, as well as their families and health professionals in the field. It is a story of the power of T'ai Chi and spiritual growth.

I am proud to have met Jason and to have witnessed his determination and his willingness to be vulnerable, as he explores the path of recovery, growth and meaning.

Alison Ryan
Clinical Psychologist in Neuropsychology
Community Head Injury Service

Foreword
by Brian Blessed

How do I possibly follow the wonderful foreword by the outstanding clinical psychologist in neuropsychology, Alison Ryan. She is a tour-de force, and I honour her. But follow I must, drawn on by my friend Jason Riddington's astonishing book.

How in the name of Heaven do I begin to describe how this work has affected me? Yes! It draws me on like some vibrating spiritual magnet invented by the Dalai Lama, and the redoubtable Shantanand Saraswati of India, and dozens of magical avatars who live in caves throughout inner Mongolia. Sorry Jason! I am almost getting out of control! After a deep breath, I will continue in the Brian Blessed way and attempt some kind of sanity.

This book is a celebration. It is a tale of extraordinary courage and sustained and tenacious bravery. Jason has determination, inner strength, a delightful sense of humour and a love for all that is worthwhile. He breaks many psychological barriers. He has no common personality. A spiritual fire burns within him and makes him lovingly formidable.

He is a terrific actor. I remember seeing him play Hamlet on stage a few years ago. He was absolutely amazing! During this period, I worked with him in the play The Lion in Winter. I played the king, Henry II, and he my son, Geoffrey. Once more, he gave a fine performance. I had the good fortune to direct him in my film King Lear. He proved to be astonishing as the villain, Edmund. Later, I directed him at the delightful theatre The Mill at Sonning in Agatha Christie's, The Hollow! Once again, he gave a gem of a performance as John Cristow.

Among his many attributes, Jason has proved to be a fine teacher. What is clear in this book is that he does not have a death wish. On the contrary, he has a life wish. His staggering tome is a clarion call to boldly go forth and fulfil your dreams. I salute him! For he is a multidimensional explorer. Intrepid explorers have always fired my imagination and left me begging for more. Such people are our dreams made flesh and blood. Jason fits the bill perfectly. His book can be compared to a symphonic poem. It is, at its heart a limitless prayer, most importantly it has hope!

Read the book, again and again and again. There is a sacred stillness at its core. It reminds me of a small section in William Wordsworth's poem "Tintern Abbey":

And I have felt
A presence that disturbs me with the joy
Of elevated thoughts; a sense sublime
Of something far more deeply interfused,
Whose dwelling is the light of setting suns,
And the round ocean and the living air,
And the blue sky, and in the mind of man:
A motion and a spirit, that impels
All thinking things, all objects of all thought,
And rolls through all things.

William Wordsworth, 1798

Wordsworth and Jason Riddington have a great deal in common.

- Brian Blessed

Part 1

Introduction

This isn't going to be an easy book to write. Not just because it outlines the devastating effects of a massive subarachnoid haemorrhage that nearly killed me, not just because it deals with the devastating effects that brain injury has upon one's physical function and mental well-being; but mainly because there is so much of what happened to me, chiefly some of the most harrowing things of which I simply have no memory. Perhaps that's a good thing? Maybe? But perhaps those terrible things need to be told, so that as full a picture as possible can be presented to you so that you know exactly what I've recovered from. Not to be in-your-face about my recovery. Far from it and actually quite the opposite; I'm in recovery and can see that this will be very lengthy process, probably lasting for the rest of my life: it's so that we can share in the ardent hope, humour and triumphs that can come from the place of worst adversity.

It's what we do so well us humans. We adapt and overcome. Therefore, I'm going to ask my dear wife Faye, who as you'll come to realise is very much a real heroine of this story, to write a chapter of her own outlining to you the bits that I've missed out. I thought this approach to be the best, so that what I share with you, no matter how inaccurate, in terms of timeline or indeed missed events, will at least be written from the heart, from within the inner world of the patient so to speak, and will be as honest an account of the events connected to my brain injury, and to the ongoing processes of my recovery, that I can give.

From the outset I want to declare to you just how difficult it is to recover from brain injury. I say this in the spirit of unity with other survivors: if you're reading this you've probably had a brain injury yourself or know someone who has; or perhaps you're interested in T'ai Chi and exploring some of the more spiritual paths that we can opt for in life. Whoever you are, I've discovered that talking about recovery from brain injury actually brings up more areas of universal concern, especially post-Covid.

The number of people who have apologised to me when learning of my brain injury after they've been stressing about their 'Covid-brain' symptoms is alarming. It seems to me that us brain injury survivors have an opportunity to lead the way with helpful advice and analysis for those in our community struggling with mental health issues be that as the result of brain injury, Covid or whatever. The symptoms are very similar, therefore so might be the solutions.

In this way outlining the obstacles encountered and the steps I've taken to attempt to overcome them, might make it so that others identify with elements that mirror their own difficulties: enabling us to explore possible modes of recovery together. In my instance I have recovered incredibly quickly from the physical disabilities, I suffered with following my SAH and subsequent meningitis infection, seizure and shunt operation; but I'm still having to recover from the injury to the brain itself which means that I'm incredibly susceptible to insomnia, brain-fog and fatigue. To those who do not understand, or who have little knowledge or experience of brain injury recovery, this can seem to be somewhat mysterious and frustrating. For all the world I seem to be normal, except for the fact that I still cannot deal with groups of people, noisy environments or making decisions!

Rather than focusing too heavily on the difficulties we face, I'm going to outline the steps that I've taken to attempt to recover from the ill-effects of my brain injury. I'm aware that my T'ai Chi training and my approaches to overcoming physical impediments are quite unusual and as such might offer a different perspective for you to explore yourselves. None of what I discuss is new, nor even very difficult to do, but might offer different approaches to potential recovery from brain injury/mental-illness/low self-esteem than you've encountered thus far. I do hope you find something in these pages to be useful and inspiring.

If you've had a brain injury and you're anything like me, your mind, your very thinking has changed. You might therefore find sustaining concentration difficult and might find holding onto specific ideas for long periods really tricky. I know I do. As such my paragraphs and chapters are kept mercifully short! Partly to help you guys get what I'm on about, and partly because my writing style, along with my thinking 'style' has become much more concise and to the point.

The print font of this book is bigger than normal to help with reading and Gregor's amazing illustrations will offer a different perspective and approach to assimilate the subject matter of the chapters. In short, you might find you get more from the artwork than you do from the words at the moment, and that's all totally cool. Think of this book more as a manual that you can dip in and out of and come back to. It's not meant to be hard work! We've been through enough!

Chapter 1
Death

WARNING; in this chapter I describe my near death experiences. Please do not read it if you are feeling fragile, or if you feel that it might conflict with your belief systems. I am not trying to convince you of anything. On the contrary I'm simply describing something that happened to me: an experience. A bit like if you were to tell me about a journey that you once went on, the journey itself is over and doesn't exist. Your memory of it, however, is real and is in existence. Therefore, the story of your journey wouldn't be up for debate, we might quibble over details in the re-telling of it, but your journey, like mine, would be yours to have experienced and its story would be yours to tell. Like mine. And these near-death experiences form such an integral part of my journey back to life that, no matter how difficult or disturbing, I believe what happened needs to be told to give the genuine spiritual framework and context to my recovery. Do with it what you will.

I suddenly felt myself fall back four times. Four sudden jerks backwards. One. Two. Three. Four. I felt it, that sickening feeling in the pit of your stomach when you have the 'falling' dream. But this was no dream. I knew that. I knew this was real, as real as it gets. I could feel it's reality. The physicality of it. The visceral plane. Everything was pitch black around me and I floated for a moment after the fourth jolt backwards. Then bright light all around me. I was still floating on my back.

And somehow next to me was a man lying on his back, motionless, facing upwards. And even though I was lying next to him I somehow looked at him from directly above him. For all the world he looked like he—and bear with me here—because I'm using words to describe what I have no previous experience of and words are limited to that which we can ascribe meaning… this is so hard to describe accurately, to get it right so that you can see what I saw and feel what I felt and experience what I experienced… I'll try. He was wearing what I can only describe as a very feathery, very black, very theatrical 'crow's' outfit. The 'beak' as such wasn't really beak-like other that it's shape for it too was covered in the black feathers, albeit they were smaller feathers than those over his torso.

Thinking about it, I only really saw his top half. The beak covered almost all of his face. No eyes, but I could see his chin, his jawline, his mouth and cheeks. He had white face-paint and upon reflection now I guess I would say he looked a little like Robert Smith from The Cure, but not really because that's just me making a connection with the known, from my teenage past, listening to The Cure and looking at the cassette album cover. It's just to give you an idea. The truth is his image remains clear to me and his isn't a face that I'd seen before, or one that I've seen since. But he did look a bit like Robert Smith, that's all…His face is also one that I'd never forget. We floated there in the white void together.

I had the residue feeling of fright from the final jolting fall still festering in my stomach. I remember I tried to straighten up and kind of flailed around in the white void unable to steady myself. His countenance was soft and gentle. He was friendly and if I had to choose an expression, I'd say he was gently smiling, although I couldn't see his upper lip that clearly as it wafted under the feathers. He remained still, as animated as I could imagine a motionless being to be. No attitude. No agenda. Just perfectly still, and perfectly friendly.

Now I'm going to tell you something, that for some reason, at this moment of writing, I haven't even told those closest to me. Not my wife. Not my children. And not my eldest daughter Emily whom this is kind of about. But these were my—ah, I'll call them thoughts—but they were more solid than that. It's like the kind of acute resonance you have in your head after a monumental event like just escaping serious injury in an accident of some sort. It lives with you.

This is what happened: I became aware of Emily who was heavily pregnant at the time and I remember saying out loud as I wobbled trying to get upright in the white void, "No! I need to meet her!" Emily had found out the sex of her baby and we were all waiting to meet *her*…baby Leila as it turns out…but at this point she was unborn and other than being female, unknown to me. But I called out that I wanted to meet her all the same.

Then the strangest thing. Really the oddest thing. I have no explanation as to why this happened and I had no preceding thought about it. I didn't see, or think, or hear anything first: suddenly the palm of my right hand slowly raised in front of my gaze, in a move that I knew well, that was second nature to me. For some reason still unknown to me, I was doing a bit of T'ai Chi Qigong—a fairly nondescript exercise from it.

Certainly not one of the more well-known moves that you might have in your mind now if you've ever done any T'ai Chi.

This is the move. Imagine yourself stood in the centre of a perfectly square empty room. You're in the middle, the four corners stretching out diagonally from you. You are the centre point. Now breathe in. On your next out—breath you will slowly lift your right-hand palm upwards tracing the left diagonal line of the room. Your arm moves as though in thick water, making the movement slow and dense. But, paradoxically, in the palm of your hand is a ball of fire. This is your chi, your life force. And you see the flames swerve and dance as you lift your hand up to the top of the corner. You feel a gentle warmth in the palm of your hand from the fire.

When it reaches the apex, you then bring the hand down whilst simultaneously bringing the left hand upwards. As the hands pass in front of you, you scoop the fire from your right palm to your left palm as it lifts upwards through the thick water. There are the flames, flickering, smoking slightly. And you breathe out…breathe in…breathe out…until the next time, and the next, and the next, and the next, and the next, and the next, and the next, and the next, and the next…you get the drift!

I tried to straighten myself, steady myself and get vertical. The wobbling started to subside. I focused on my palms more and more, slowly rising and falling in the foreground. In front of me now, behind my burning palms, in the background, was the odd friendly crow-man figure, still lying motionless but so very, very alive. I continued with the T'ai Chi move.

Then I opened my eyes and I was in hospital. The doctors told me I nearly died.

Two or three days later I had a serious relapse. I'd contracted meningitis and was rushed into emergency surgery.

And I experienced the exact, same, precise thing. Millisecond by millisecond the absolute carbon-copy, identical, visceral, physical experience.

Then I opened my eyes and I was in hospital.
The doctors told me I nearly died.
Twice.

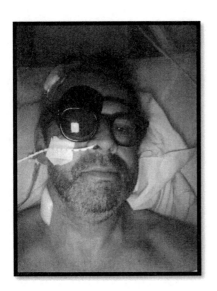 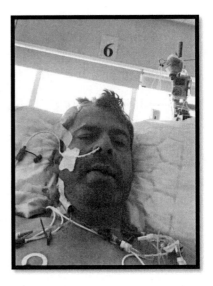

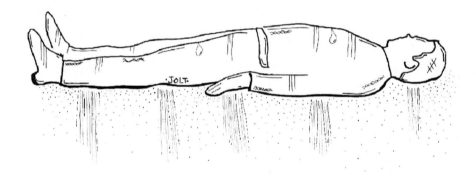

Chapter 2
What the F*** Happened?

I'm not fully sure even now of what happened, but I'll try to get it as accurate as I can. June 27th, 2021, I went for a bike ride hill training up 'Whiteleaf' a challenging hill in the Chilterns where I live. Now do bear in mind, that for me, and I'm not saying this to brag, but for me, who has had a lifetime of road cycling and climbed massive tour mountains in the Pyrenees such as the Col d'Aubisque (where I once owned an apartment for the purpose of skiing for the kids and bike training for me), the Col de Marie Blanc (the steepest), the Col du Pourtelet (the longest), the Col du Tourmelet (the highest) etc etc, and all take hours of gruelling, grinding pushing up, ever up all exceeding climbs of1800m. So 'Whiteleaf' for me was nothing. I hit the gradient and struggled. I mean really struggled. I found my easiest gear and couldn't believe how I struggled.

Another cyclist cruised by. 'What's wrong with me?' I asked myself. I got to the top and a female cyclist asked if I was, ok? 'Yes fine!' I snapped—my ego bruised. I descended barely able to keep it together. I cycled to the yard where we have our horses (my wife's a show jumper…much more about horses…and dogs later) in Butlers Cross just a few miles from the bottom of that climb. I gave them their hay and dinners, mucked them out whilst feeling rotten. I had this massive headache at the back of my head and felt sick. I thought it was altitude sickness coming back (I'd suffered when in the high Pyrenees many moons ago), but I ploughed on. I got back on the bike to cycle the 10 flat miles home. I was going at a snail's pace. Head pounding and I felt sick, so very nauseous.

About a mile or so from home I got off the bike and threw up on the side of the road. I struggled into the house and was violently ill. I went up to bed taking paracetamol. I continued to be sick all night.

June 29, 2021. The next day I felt better and I drove to pick my youngest daughter Phoebe up from her mum's home in Bedford to drop her off at school (she was a boarder at Tring Park just down the road from me in Aylesbury). Having dropped her off I drove back home. Then I woke in hospital two days later.

Here's what happened as told by my dear wife Faye who saved my life. I got in and Faye heard a sickening thud. I had collapsed, hitting my mouth on a radiator in the hall way as I went down. She heroically performed CPR (among her many talents she's a brilliantly successful personal trainer and knows First Aid, she also, appallingly, saw an old boyfriend collapse with a sudden cardiac arrest, unfortunately he lost his life in hospital a few days later). She kept me alive doing CPR whilst calling the emergency services. They arrived and gave me an adrenaline shot and kept me going whilst rushing me to John Radcliffe hospital in Oxford. I was put into an induced coma as it was a Sunday night until the next morning when the neuroscience team performed emergency surgery for a massive subarachnoid haemorrhage, saving my life. They had put a drain in the top of my skull to drain the blood from my brain and I was put in the Intensive Care Unit — all tubes and monitors.

The following couple of days I came round and was doing well, until Faye noticed that I was incoherent much of the time. She raised the alarm and I was treated for a meningitis infection and operated upon again as I had a life-threatening seizure. They gave me a spinal-tap a nightmare gravitational drain that comes out of your spine to allow the excess blood-soaked fluid to slowly drip, drip from the brain, a kind of continual epidural, and if you forget you have it and move too quickly to the toilet for example it could be catastrophic. The surgeons told me I nearly died again! Thank God for Faye, that's all I can say!

When I came round again, I had some paralysis in my right foot, I'd had a bleed on my retina and couldn't see very much out of my right eye as well as having Terson Syndrome (double vision). My hearing had been affected terribly —I assume from the drugs they gave for meningitis—and everything sounded like it was being played on devilish, ghostly cathedral bells: really scary and disconcerting. Ultimately after numerous lumber punctures to drain excess fluid that was persistently building up in my brain causing acute almost instantaneous memory loss, the decision was made to have further brain surgery to insert a shunt (invented by Roald Dahl for his daughter who suffered with hydrocephalus) a permanent valve that drains the excess fluid from my brain into my stomach…

But before that, when I was first in hospital, the brain injury and regimen of pain killers — morphine, three hours later, codeine, three hours later paracetamol etc etc and anti-seizure medication, the anti-biotic, and blood thinning medication made me hallucinate. I believed I was in a very badly acted reality TV show. Kind of like the Truman Show but set in a hospital and I believed the staff were part of a giant conspiracy to imprison me and experiment upon me. One wonderful nurse got the full brunt of my paranoia when she gave me my meds. I just didn't believe her performance. "No one is that nice!" I yelled and pretended to take the meds. Bad idea! I was bad. Really, really ill. And so very close to death.

That was the start of my month-long recovery in the High Care Unit at John Radcliffe hospital. Unbeknown to me I was in one of the best facilities in the world, with a neurosurgery team of world-class doctors and nurses. And that really is the start of my story. The start of an incredible journey back to life.

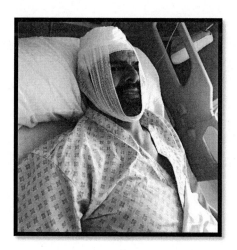 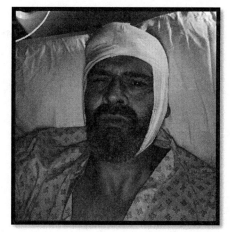

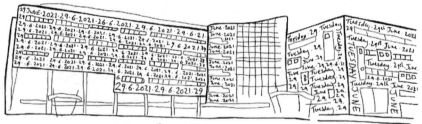

TUESDAY. 29th. JUNE. 2021.

Chapter 3
Hospital—My Inner World

Hospital, especially in 2021 when Covid was at its height, was a bizarre place to be. The oddity of your life depending upon the help of total strangers in masks, often with thick incomprehensible accents made the extremity of my situation intensely frustrating as well as profoundly isolating. My medication was given every 3 hours. And before it was administered, I would be asked things like, "How are you today, Jason?", "Do you know where you are?", "What day is it today?" and so on. The critical care unit on the neuroscience ward at John Radcliffe Hospital was where my days and nights were spent, unable to see clearly, or hear clearly and unable to walk except when aided by one of the greatest men I have had the pleasure to get to know, Sri the porter who stood over my bed at night, who washed me, who talked when I couldn't — ah the list goes on of what he did for me, who helped me to shuffle to the toilet — all tubes and drips going with me…

Anyway, it was in these first few weeks, when I was desperately ill that I really started to live inwardly. Let me explain. I began to think really deeply about the nature of self. I kept wondering who exactly the doctors and nurses were talking to when asking me how I was feeling, or getting along. Obviously, I know they were asking me, but I began to think a lot about the very nature, or essence of 'me', and let's face it I had a lot of thinking time! For example, for me to be able to answer the "how are you today" question I kind of had to divide

27

myself in two. There was the me that was asking the question "how am I?" and there was the me that was the subject of that question. Now when you're ill. I mean when you know you're close to death ill, this sense of duality becomes critically important.

Because if you identify entirely with the illness, with the part of you that's so close to destroying you then you're sunk. I somehow knew this instinctively; I think we all do. And maybe it's that awareness of self that makes human beings so unique. I mean it's pretty trippy but true that in order to answer the "how are you" question a different me has to ask the question to the one that is lying there critically ill following a massive brain injury. It's almost like the question is being asked of the captain of a ship, a kind of esoteric vessel that we (our souls?) drive, or guide and are given a kind of stewardship over for the duration of our lifetime. The "how are you" question in the hospital critical care unit is really a status report of the damage done to the vessel and how repairs are coming along. You are being asked about you.

Yes. But in order to answer the question you must separate from the physical you. And in the case of a brain injury, you have to separate from the physical you and the you that is the brain in order to consider the question of how well or otherwise you are. So where is this other you to be found if not in the body or the brain? Let's consider this question a little deeper.

Imagine we're back in the white room we did some T'ai Chi in together in Chapter 1. Imagine you're standing in the centre of a perfectly square white room. Everything is white — the floor, the ceiling, the door, the window-sills, the walls. All is white and empty. Now let's play a little game. You might remember this rhyme from your childhood. Point to the ceiling, point to the floor, point to the window, point to the door. Game over…point to the room. You see you can't can you? When you try you realise that you point at a wall, or the ceiling, or the door, but pointing at the room is actually impossible.

So where is the room? If you can't point to it does it exist? Well yes, we're standing in the room so its existence is real enough, but what, if it can't be pointed to, or touched or even seen as a separate entity, what is the room? Is it an amalgamation of all of the separate entities that we can see and touch, the walls, floor and so on? Is it a sum of all of the parts that make a whole room? Is it an agreed collective consciousness that represents a concept that we've learned to recognise as a room, even though only part of the physical properties of the room can be touched and interacted with (the walls, floor ceiling and so on)? Let's let those questions linger for a while and think of the room in a slightly different way.

What if the room is you? I mean what if we just exchange the word 'room' for the word 'you' and all that that means therein. Aren't the two things incredibly alike? If we played the same pointing game, you can indeed point to parts of you, your chest, a leg, your head, your nose…but try pointing to the whole you. Things get tricky there, don't they? You'll obviously end up pointing to bits of you, but identifying the whole you and pointing to it is impossible. And yet… And yet…That's the part that was being asked that question, "how are you?" When you're bed-ridden with an acute brain injury these are the kinds of thoughts that occupy the mind, wherever that is.

At least that was the case with me. And here's another thought. If, going back to the room for a minute, one of the walls was cracked, had subsidence and was defective in some way wouldn't it be an extraordinary thing if the whole room consciousness was able to somehow heal, to mend, to fix by some magic—all-by-itself the broken wall?

Well, I can tell you from experience that that's what happens with us. Somehow our cracked and damaged walls repair themselves. But why do some people repair better than others? And in the case of brain injury, if the organ that does the thinking is itself injured, where, or what is the thing that heals it? Where were my inner thoughts and feelings coming from as I lay half-dead and brain injured on that bed? And why, after the two occasions that I almost died did the medics all tell me how strong I was? How strong my will to survive was? Where is this strength? Where is the will? Certainly not in my damaged body or brain. So perhaps somewhere where the wholeness resides? Somewhere other than the body, or the brain? If that's where the will to survive resides, where inner strength lives then it's pretty reasonable to also say it's also where love is, but also where fear can reside: in the wholeness, the consciousness, oneness or spirit?

Fear of death was very real for me. But more real was the near-death experience I'd undergone, twice. More real was this strange inner world I was inhabiting in which I was beginning to understand the nature of things. The many, many twists and turns between life and death, and the endless journeying that our wholeness, or consciousness, or whatever it is that we are, goes on.

Lying immobile in that hospital bed, barely able to move, I began regular T'ai Chi Qigong sessions…in my mind. And that, let me tell you, that is meditation.

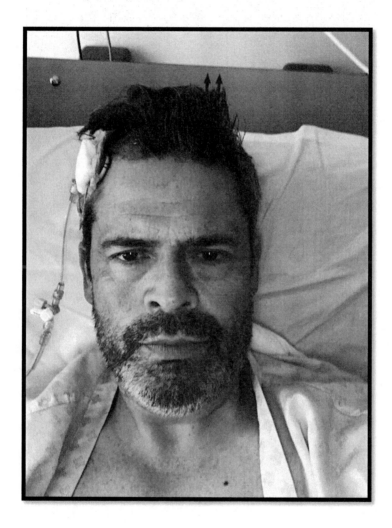

Chapter 4
Learning to Meditate

It's pretty ironic, at least I find it pretty ironic, that I've often said, in retrospect in a pretty thoughtless macho kind of way, that if I ever got incarcerated (and by that I imagine some kind of padded cell isolation, not the sort with huge fellas that beat you senseless and get you to pick up the soap in the showers if you get my drift!) that I would come out of it fitter and stronger than when I went in because I have, and have always had throughout my adult life, T'ai Chi. Or to give the form that I do its proper title T'ai Chi Qigong. Now let's be clear about this. I'm no guru or spiritualist, I'm not even what I would class as a martial artist in the sense that I don't attend T'ai Chi class or anything like that. I was just taught this stuff at drama school, was reminded of it by my son's martial art teacher Roberto Parisi when he was little and I've just kind of refined it and stuck with it ever since.

The Qigong that I do consists of three sections. The first is all about breathing and relaxation and has all of the slow graceful moves that you'd recognise as T'ai Chi. Section two is about stretching, deep stretching and section three is about strength and has poses that you'd recognise as done by Shaolin kung-fu monks if you've ever seen them warm up, except without holding massive clay pots in each hand as you do it, or breaking said pots with your head etc! None of that for me! It gets progressively more taxing as you go along, and is fair to say that it really does, through repetition, get you very strong and very flexible. It's also pretty boring as it's the same (strictly the same) every time you do it. Which is great from the perspective of learning it, but tough to maintain as its always the same. Except for, of course, the other key elements to T'ai Chi which are the breathing and visualisation you do whilst doing each move. They make it really fascinating.

I touched on it in Chapter 1, and it goes something like this: for each move there is an in breath and an out breath that corresponds to the physical movement, and along with that you visualise fire balls in the palm of your hand. Depending on the move you might exchange the fire from one hand to the other but whatever happens there is a constant flow of fire and breathing. All this whilst, paradoxically feeling and visualising your limbs pushing the moves through thick water. For the whole of section one the legs are bent and as you get stronger the bend gets deeper and the moves more dynamic. So, in fact, even though the moves remain the same on the surface, on a deeper level they are always evolving as you get stronger and deeper into the breathing and visualisations. This is what is meant by Chi, the flow of life force, and this is how the same set of moves can last you a lifetime—always moving and evolving, like life itself.

So, what's this 'irony' I started talking to you about? Well, the irony is that although I was indeed incarcerated in the ICU ward of John Radcliffe hospital, I was also incarcerated in my own body. I could barely move a muscle. Let's be clear I was pretty screwed for the first three of my four weeks there. I had paralysis in my right foot, my right eye from the bleed on my retina was causing appalling double vision and I wore a patch over it, I had appalling headaches and my hearing (I assumed from the drugs to counter the meningitis) was terrible, listening to music was like listening to demonic cathedral bells, there was no bass at all, just this terrible unrecognisable shrill tolling of bells—it was heart-breaking.

I've been a music buff all my life, my youngest daughter Phoebe and I (she's an unbelievably talented singer/dancer/actor currently studying musical theatre at Urdang in London) have spent endless hours listening to different bands and styles of music, dissecting the form and structure (I did music A level) identifying instruments and so on. So, for me the loss of hearing was truly horrific. Add to that my ridiculous double vision! Oh, and I had a catheter fitted for about the first ten days, so the only time I got to move from my bed was when I needed a 'number two' and that took the help of Sri and a couple of other nurses as I hobbled along with my various drips and tubes…a sorry state indeed!

So anyway, in my state of internal incarceration I started to do something quite odd. I gave myself the challenge of doing all three sections of T'ai Chi Qigong in my head. I had to breathe along with each move, and if I lost focus and my mind drifted off the task in hand I'd have to start again. Not a bad game to play to pass the incessant turbulent pain-filled hours as it turned out. To begin with I was hopeless, I couldn't get past the first move (each move is repeated twelve times by the way). Then I got in a panic because I couldn't remember the next move. I calmed down and managed to string two moves together, then three, then four. Then I realised I didn't have any fire in my palms! Back to the beginning! And on and on this went.

Hour after hour... Of course, I did have my phone in hospital, and I would FaceTime Faye, the kids, or my brother when strong enough with carefully rehearsed moments to make everyone think I was ok. In fact, a word about 'stuff' whilst we're on the subject: when all is said and done and you end up on the hospital ward, or just sat in a chair, as we all inevitably will end up, you realise just how little 'stuff' you really need. Pyjamas and slippers are nice, a phone, my brother Ryan got me this very cool bendy phone holder that attached to my bed trolley, I had earphones, ear plugs (all to try to deal with the hearing issues) and a toothbrush. That's it! So really stuff is just that...stuff. Don't get stressed or worried about things that ultimately you won't give a monkey's butt about! It's just stuff! Of course, I also had my daily visits from my incredible life-saver wife Faye (this was when Covid was rife so she was the only person allowed to visit me) but for the rest of the time, when conscious, I tried to do T'ai Chi in my head.

So, here's the strange thing, I got stronger and stronger at doing T'ai Chi in my mind. Long before any physical recovery, I was able to shut my eyes and do a fully focused, concentrated T'ai Chi session (the whole thing only lasts 45 minutes at most) in my mind. At will. I could just get into it and go from start to finish, full-on seeing myself on this grassy mound, in front of a vast horizon of a setting sun, with real fire burning in each palm, smoking as I moved, breathing, each move the deepest and most dynamic I'd ever done...all in my mind.

Now I don't know about you, but if you're anything like me you'll have tried to meditate before. I've read books on it, listened to pod casts, watched Buddhist monks on YouTube all to no avail. If I tried to think of nothing, I'd inevitably think of something, or be aware of my own thinking, which creates more thinking! I've tried to focus on the breath going in and out of my nostrils and I last about two seconds! Agghgghggg it's soooo hard! But, because I've pretty much always done T'ai Chi (except when injured, most recently from a car accident a few years ago which caused terrible lower back pain and I stupidly as it turns out, did no T'ai Chi for months and took pain-killers.

Here's a fact, I haven't drunk alcohol for 24 years because I'm an alcoholic, I have an addictive composition which makes me susceptible to chemical addiction. Yes, you've guessed it, I became addicted to the prescription meds with my back injury and as you'll read later here, I had evil withdrawals, when I eventually got home, from the necessary courses of morphine and codeine that I was on in hospital. It's also possible that the brain aneurism itself was caused by the car accident, or from birth…it was some kind of head trauma that caused it in the first place, I was in hospital because the aneurysm had burst…)

What was I saying? Ah yes, because I've pretty much always done T'ai Chi, I've contented myself that with the visualisation and peaceful aspect of it that it's a kind of meditation even if you are moving, albeit slowly and gracefully…so what does it matter if I can't meditate! I'm kind of meditating when I do T'ai Chi! But this new form of mind T'ai Chi got me thinking. Isn't this actual pucker meditating?! I mean who the hell knows what any meditation master is actually thinking anyway?

As far as I was concerned, I was fully focused, awake and fully present for each moment of each move, the bonus being that T'ai Chi comes to an end. I'm aware through so much repetition of where each move in the whole sequence lies and where I am in terms of time. And it's this awareness of myself in my mind doing T'ai Chi within the flow of time that gave me the absolute sense of successfully meditating. And it became my thing. My private thing. When things were looking pretty bleak, I could do my T'ai Chi meditation and for all the world I swear I would feel in my body as if I'd done the session for real.

I'm now certain that discovering meditation (or at least my version of it) in this way helped in my recovery. Some years ago, I read this incredible book on meditation by Jon Kabat-Zinn in which he likens meditation to a pot that's on the stove. By focusing attention moment by moment to what is present and happening right now and not on the pot failing to boil; instead of projecting frustrations at what is not happening ('a watched pot never boils!'), we begin to enjoy the journey of each microsecond the boiling pot becoming a by-product of the time well spent.

So, if meditation shifts our consciousness towards the here and now away from what is not happening, then for those of us recovering from brain injury I reckon by shifting our consciousness to the here and now (in my case visualising T'ai Chi) away from the physical and emotional devastation wrought by brain injury, it actually allows the body to heal itself… as it naturally does. Like the wall in the room magically fixing itself, this is what we are designed to do if we can release ourselves from the anguish of focusing upon what is wrong with us. No matter how great that might be.

I know there's been a few raised medical eyebrows at the speed of my physical recovery: my hearing returned to pretty normal, albeit with occasional tinnitus, after a few weeks, my paralysis went before I left hospital and my eyesight returned to normal (I'll tell you more about this later) after a couple of months.

As soon as I was able, probably after three weeks or so, I got the wonderful Sri to take me and my drip to a place in the ward that was quiet and I could attempt T'ai Chi for real. I was this decrepit, thin, pained figure at that point, shuffling along the hallway, Sri holding me up under my arm, wheeling the drip along.

And let me tell you, after three weeks in a hospital bed and with the effects of the terrible brain injury it took me an age just to walk the fifteen feet or so to the quiet spot with Sri ready to catch me at any point. And when I started the first T'ai Chi moves I was shocked at just how weak and inflexible my body had become. Everything hurt, it was agony. And there was this really disconcerting lag between thinking of the move and getting my limbs to move. It was like the connections were missing or slightly off. I felt like quitting I was so utterly devastated that my physicality had abandoned me so quickly and so radically.

Then I heard from Sri, "Come on Mr Jason, you got this!" his wonderful Keralan politeness and dauntless encouragement kind of shamed me into pushing through the pain and frustration. Sri started filming on my phone for me still issuing encouraging instruction, ready to pounce and catch me at any point if I fell… and I did it. Just section one, very badly and it probably lasted ten minutes max, but I did it. A positive Facebook post! Yay!

And that was the start of the physical recovery. That first T'ai Chi session on the hospital ward set me on the bumpy twisty but relatively fast (so I'm told by the medics who look after me still) road to physical recovery. I keep on saying 'physical' because my mental recovery has been less straight-forward, in fact it's been turbulent and is still ongoing. I guess I've got PTSD and I'm so very lucky to have the help and support of Faye and a friend who's become a councillor who is brilliant for me, and the fantastic psychology team supplied by our extraordinary NHS. I'll talk much more about mental health later.

41

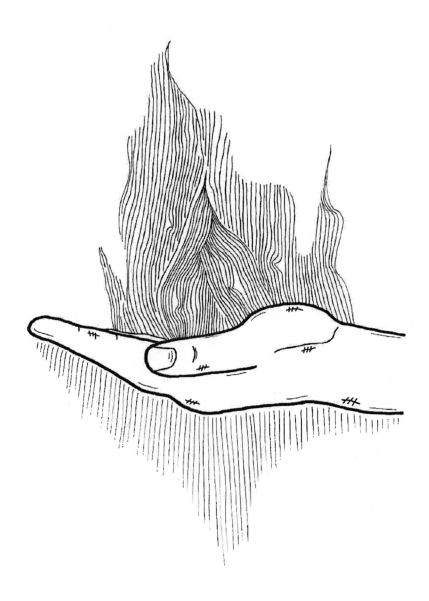

Chapter 5
Hearing Loss

In a way, at first, as odd as this sounds, I was glad to suffer from hearing loss. My dear son Mikey was born profoundly deaf as a result of Usher's Syndrome and I've always had this fury with God or the unearthly powers-that-be that you turn to, or on, when you're faced with extremities in life to blame or to question. My biggest thing was why him and not me? As a parent you'd take a bullet for your child, so to see him having to overcome such an enormous disability made me so mad that I couldn't take it from him and bear the load myself. Now I was getting to experience perhaps something of what he has had to endure (admirably as it turns out for this incredible young man, now 25, hears with the use of a cochlear implant and has amazing speech. It took years of hard work, but he did it!)

Anyway, as I say, at first, I was in martyr mode: but eventually the demonic bells starting to take their toll on me pardon the pun! It was driving me mental. Every loud noise, the TV from an adjacent ward, anything would seemingly set off the bells of doom and I could do nothing to stop them or escape their monotonous tortuous intrusion.

In the end I decided, much like the mind T'ai Chi meditation that I was mastering, that I had to train, or rather, re-train my hearing. I thought the best approach was to limit the amount of sound and to listen to something that I knew so that I could try to force myself to hear things as I knew they should be. Finding the right stimulus took an age. Faye had bought me these great earbuds that connected to my phone, but any attempt to listen to music just overwhelmed and depressed me. So I decided instead to watch a film that I knew well where the sound track was well known to me but not so obtrusive as to make me give up and give in to the hearing loss.

After a number of attempts I settled on True Grit, the Coen brother's remake. I love this film both the original John Wayne version and the Coen brother's homage to it with Jeff Bridges playing the irascible drunken Rooster Cogburn. The other thing that I really liked was, like me at this point, Rooster is one-eyed and wears a patch, which kind of made me feel like I could still be cool even if my eyesight remained as it was!

Night after night I would watch the same section of the film where there was non-diegetic sound of Western music and replay it again and again trying to force my brain to hear the whole score as I knew it should sound. Sometimes I think I thought I heard the right sounds, but most of the time it was muffled by the demonic bells. But eventually, after three weeks or so of trying it worked. Indeed, it was an overnight thing. I woke up and the bells were gone and I could hear clearly again! I played so much music, listened to Phoebe's singing with tears of joy streaming down my face. I couldn't believe it! I was like Scrooge the day after he's been visited by the spirits and he starts afresh on his new life journey.

It took me some days to fully come to terms with regaining my hearing after such a turbulent time. I was left with some tinnitus, which I'm told is probably due to the necessary anti-seizure medication I'm currently on. I had a hearing test a few weeks ago and remarkably my hearing is within 10% of an 18-year-old perfect hearing!

My eyesight issues took longer to resolve and needed some novel and radical approaches to fix!

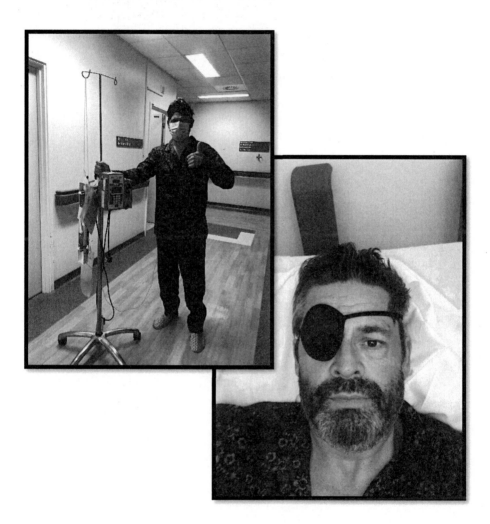

Chapter 6
Home – The Hardest Journey of them All

My dear reader, I'm afraid these next few chapters are going to be pretty bleak, dark and full of terror.

I think both Faye and I had the notion that when it was time for me to leave hospital, I would be better, or pretty close to fully recovered. This was, to be fair, in spite of the fact that surgeons and nurses had said throughout that the recovery from my brain injury would be long and difficult. I guess we were both pretty naive. The truth is that when I left hospital on July 29, 2021, a full month after my admission, I'd been through what I now know to have been one of the most extreme cases to have survived. Most don't. Of those who have a bleed on the brain due to a burst aneurysm like mine only 10% survive. Of that 10% most are left with some critical medical conditions such as paralysis, or chronic cognitive deficiencies. And of that 10% who survive the first few days, those, like me, who develop a meningitis infection of the brain rarely live to tell the tale.

During the month in hospital, I'd had four surgeries. First the emergency coil to stop the aneurysm from bleeding which was done by keyhole surgery through the groin. Next was when they made a hole in my skull and fitted a drain to remove the blood. Next was the spinal tap fitted to again drain the blood from the fluid on my brain. Finally, as the fluid on the brain could not be stabilised and I had hydrocephalus requiring endless epidurals, they fitted a shunt.

This device (invented by the extraordinary Roald Dahl for his daughter who suffered from hydrocephalus) is a valve that takes excess fluid from the brain and deposits it via a tube that runs under the skin down my neck, across my chest and into my tummy. Pretty major stuff, this last procedure is apparently very hard to get right. My wonderful consultant Mr Griffiths telling me: "There's no such thing as a perfect shunt"! But they did get it right! And on the 29th July, two days after shunt surgery, still feeling sick from the aesthetic, battered and bruised, unable to see straight and with a splitting headache, I was discharged from John Radcliffe hospital.

They packed me off with codeine and paracetamol for the inevitable dreadful headaches, and laxatives to counter the constipating effects of the codeine. I remember I had a real sense of trepidation to be leaving the safety of the ward as I staggered along the walls with Faye under one shoulder leading me out. This frail, hobbling figure, who couldn't see two paces in front of him without flailing his arms out at what he thought were objects in the way so profoundly disturbing was the double vision, was not the conquering heroic figure I'd pictured when imagining this day.

As I left the ward I felt utterly defeated as well as being terrified by the terrible vision issues I was left with. I tried to put a brave face on for Faye, who was asking repeatedly if I was, ok? I was, in the main, silent. Trapped inside a broken body with a broken brain for company. I couldn't think. I couldn't get my brain to turn over. It was like I was stuck in a terrible, helpless limbo. And I was scared.

Faye sat me down on a bench just outside as she went to fetch the car over to me. The soothing sun of a summer that I'd missed was pulsating and dazzling, but it was so nice to be finally outside. She opened the passenger door and I struggled in, barely missing hitting my head (in fact it's just odd how many times I've hit my head getting into a car since this brain injury! Why would that be?). Keeping the patch over my right eye made my left (good) eye weep for some reason so I kept both eyes open, tormenting myself with the double vision, which was like seeing a second image crookedly half-overlaid onto the first.

As we set off the lines on the road flew across the windscreen and the cars on the opposite side seemed to be coming directly at us. I flinched and fidgeted. Poor Faye, to have experienced such terrible and dramatic things and to be left with this crazed maniac for her 'better' husband. She asked repeatedly if I was ok. "I'm fine darling" I closed my eyes and tried to breathe and do my T'ai Chi meditation. The traffic was terrible for some reason, Faye was so frustrated wanting to get me back as soon as she could "It's never been this bad and I've done this journey every single day!"

"I'm fine darling" breathe, T'ai Chi, breathe…

When we finally arrived home and Faye helped me out of the car, I was struck by how geometrical our new estate was. I'd never noticed before. All these straight lines, walls on top of walls, criss-crossing each other in a distressing visual helter-skelter both numbing and aching my head. The dogs (our lovely cocker spaniels Millie and Mabel) were at Faye's mum and dad's, she didn't want to overwhelm me. We staggered into the front room and I lay on the sofa, my head pounding. I can't remember when the dogs were brought over but I do remember the older dog Millie coming in very gingerly and coming over to me so quietly obviously aware of just how ill I was. She tenderly licked my fingers somehow containing her excitement. I felt like I was an alien in a world I no longer recognised. None of this was what I'd imagined when dreaming of the day I got home.

But Faye and the dogs were there and perfect. The problem was me. I couldn't see them. I couldn't access things or people anymore. I couldn't process sights or sounds or smells of anything familiar anymore. I was different. It was like I was gone and in my place was a cowering, trembling creature. I missed the morphine. Morphine makes you brave I thought. And in that terrible moment I realised that on top of everything I'd become addicted to the painkillers. I knew from experience that when the time came the withdrawals from this would be horrendous.

I took my codeine and tried to get comfortable on the sofa, the metal clip stitches in my skull from the recent surgery were tight and uncomfortable. Now what? I stroked the heads of the dogs as they sat dutifully by me. Faye stroked my head and we both cried. I wanted to be the old me, to make things better for her, but I just didn't know how. Everything was overwhelming and I was frozen in a paralysis of fear and pain.

Chapter 7
Night Terrors – Making Friends with the Crow-Man

The first month or so back home was unbelievably hard. It wasn't just the physical difficulties of my eyesight plagued as it was by double-vision, nor the constant headaches, body aches, and the general wear-and-tear after four lots of brain surgery; but it was the mental recovery that seemed so terribly far from my grasp. A few hours into the day I would be struck by what I called 'my rubber head', where an image of a chicken type head made of rubber would possess my mind and would render thinking impossible. I could barely move a step in that state and I would cry in shame at the terror I felt. I just couldn't get my brain to 'turn over'; as if I lacked the mental capacity to get the engine of my brain to run again, I would stall, stuck in the midst of whatever it was I was attempting.

I wasn't just trapped inside a broken body, but I was with a mind out of control, or rather, I was controlled by a mind so damaged that it was out to get me. It had tried to kill me in every way possible in the hospital, but now I was at home, and away from the constant care of the hospital ICU I was easy prey. That's how it felt. That's how it was. I could barely look at Faye, so riddled with fear I was that anything, even the slightest chink of love would weaken me and I would be taken back to the brink and to death. I couldn't cope with being at home, too many straight lines that converged over each other with the double-vision, and it was too much to expect Faye to cope with alone, so we decamped to the more rural setting of Faye's mum and dads house a few miles away from us.

Jean and Roger Semon, Faye's mum and dad have been incredible. The love, patience and kindness they have shown throughout this ordeal has been extraordinary.

My night terrors at this time were profound. I remember one where I was convinced my lips were glued together and I couldn't breathe, I had crushing headaches and every time I tried to sleep, I experienced the falling back sensation I described in Chapter 1 in my near death experience and would startle back into consciousness. And whether conscious or semi-conscious I would see the same image over and over of the man lying flat in the white void wearing the crow's outfit. I would get closer and closer, able to see hairline cracks in his white faceprint, his black stubble piercing through like sticks in snow. I thought he was death. And I thought he had come for me. I felt like having to go with him was inevitable. I just didn't have the strength to resist.

The only times in the day I felt ok and safe was when I was struggling through my T'ai Chi sessions. I don't know for sure if it's the regulated breathing, or the movement, or the flexibility and strength it engenders, but when doing T'ai Chi I felt closer to life than to death. Maybe the repetitive movements help in the reformation of damaged neural pathways? Perhaps just doing something was better than cowering in fear on the sofa? Or, could it be that T'ai Chi is a truly spiritual activity and as such would illicit some kind of respect from the Crow-man for during those training times he kept his distance from me. Until the night…

I don't know for how long I endured this paranormal torture. It felt like an eternity of nightly terror: I would fall asleep, fall back three times, see the Crow-man and startle awake. Over and over and over and over… I didn't know how to describe it and didn't want to scare Faye so kept it to myself as best I could.

At some point though I decided I needed to take action. That's when for the first time I put together the meditation technique I'd developed in hospital of running the whole of Qigong in my head, with my nemesis, the Crow-man. I distinctly remember saying to myself, the only way to survive is to make friends with him. Somehow, maybe because he left me in peace during T'ai Chi, or because I was clinging to the power of Chi and the spirituality it gave me, or simply because I was too afraid to do anything else; but somehow, I put the two together and believed that the Crow-man would either let me live and breathe or I'd be taken and die. But at least if I could sustain doing the entirety of Qigong, right next to him, at least I'd then be with him for long enough to get know his intentions, or to fight him somehow. Or die.

I decided that night to stay up all night if necessary, doing T'ai Chi in my mind with the Crow-man next to me, in the netherworld between states of consciousness, until it was over one way or another. And here's the funny thing, and it's something I draw great comfort from these days, and when on the rare occasions I speak of it, sweet tears of profound gratitude fall from my eyes; the funny thing is he just smiled! I stayed with him all night, doing T'ai Chi again and again in the white void with him lying next to me as before, but now, because we were together with nowhere else to go, we just dwelt in a kind of mutual sense of peace, tranquillity and joy. I still can't tell you about the Crow-man's identity, or purpose but I can tell you that I stayed with him for long enough to know that his intentions were only full of love.

From that moment on all fear of death left me. I'm not saying I haven't experienced the profound mental difficulties of brain fog, brain-fatigue that all of us brain injury survivors suffer with to varying degrees of severity, because I have and do suffer, terribly. Even though my physical recovery has been extraordinary (something that I and a growing number in the medical community put down to T'ai Chi), I still experience the crushing fatigue of brain overload and the imbalance of defunct neural inhibitors that allow too much light and sound and send me over the edge. But and this is a very big but, I have made friends, and I mean real solid there when I need him friends with the Crow-man that has put fear of death out of the equation. I'm scared of many things: of losing my recovery, scared of physical incapacity returning, but fear of death has gone.

So, who is the Crow-man? I honestly don't know for sure. He's with me all the time these days, in the background and I'll often think of him when I'm in need of comfort! How ironic! I think he's like a link, or a guide between life and death. I don't think I went too far down the death pathway if I'm honest, because I was with him. It stalled things enough for me to come back on the two occasions I nearly died and the rest of the time I just think he was giving me the opportunity to chill out with him if I wanted to. You see, honestly, there's nothing to fear. Everything is still and placid and peaceful. And look, there we are, us three, you, me and him doing T'ai Chi in front of a beautiful sunset on top of a grassy mound.

Chapter 8
Drugs—The Withdrawals that Kill

It's really common to suffer from sleep difficulties following a brain injury. Indeed, I've read and been told by the medical and psychological experts that I'm blessed to have looking after my recovery, that sleep issues and brain fatigue are the most common complaint for brain injury survivors. Withdrawals from pain-killer addiction is **not** that! It is a category of pain and anguish all of its own. It is not insomnia; it is a nightly fidgety death. Second by agonising second you silently scream for the end.

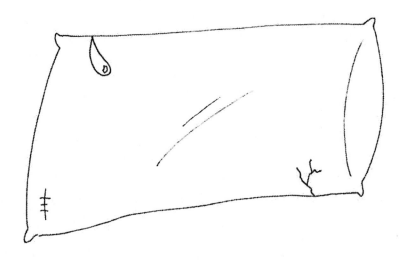

Chapter 9
Night-time Poetry

The withdrawals from prescription chemical addiction are worse than when I gave up drinking some 24 years ago. This has happened to me three times now. The first two, relatively and comparatively mild from codeine addiction following my car accident six years ago that left me rigid with lower back pain. But this last, when I came out of hospital and came off codeine and morphine was honestly like a nightly hell. It is no surprise to me that so many people are in the grip of addiction to painkilling meds, the good that they do (in my case entirely necessary to recover from brain surgery) seems to pale into nothing when compared to the appalling symptoms of withdrawal.

Each night, for the first six weeks after leaving hospital was filled with jitters, shivers, headaches and the blackest of thoughts. A living death: beyond pain and suffering. You're entirely on your own here, and only time and getting through it will be your saviour. During these lonely nights I would resort to writing poetry as a vain means of distilling some of the anguish into some representation of what it is to go through withdrawals like this. Here are the poems. Make of them what you will. They are what I wrote when in the grip of a despair that defies description. Under such circumstances the distillation of pain and suffering into these poems makes sense to me now, although at the time of writing they were a frail and dismal cry for help in the thickening shades of the night…

Accidental Poetry

I was going to let this go, you see
But I can't. It's just too in me
To let me be free, you, see?
I mean I've tried herbal tea
And meditating,
But I still have this feeling,
This thing that's making
Me sleepless and tired
Beyond capacity for rational thought, I lie here…
And I wish the dreams would come.

Bleak night

Bleak night,
Pitch dark
Fork tongued
Groove lost
Found glove
Lost love
Silence-less
Trigger point?
Lost light
Bleak night.
Return-less
Iron sheet
Lost
Alone
Beat
Electric

Blue

Sight…

Bleak night.

Pill-gone

Done

One

Flow-low-slow-low-angel-less

Fog

Fire

Lift entire

Night less

Lightless

Confess…

It's turning on myself

It's making me deranged

It does it to me

It sees right through me.

Holy God please save me. Please.

Please save me.

Bleak night….

Blindfold me. Please.

And it wasn't long before I turned away from that light that had saved me.

Not unlike but quite unlikely like a moth to the flame,

I've become buried in an earnest disease of shattered dreams,

And beacons of angst.

Against the wall I stand.

Blindfold me. Please.

Let me leave the shattered dreams with some shred of mercy please?

Some dignity?

But no.

Instead, be grateful to have all that you've got you lucky thing!

Give me something to dull the razor-sharp edge upon which I potter about.

Like a clown made-up in an empty tent

Like a man whose lost his eyes but still asks…

Blindfold me. Please.

His Boots Were Too Big

His boots were too big,

The children said of

The old man who fell that day.

How could he have walked from A to B? Let alone have lived to eighty-three?

With boots that size it's no surprise

He met with such a sudden demise.

And landed dead. Square on his head. His boots sticking out like tombstones.

Cheese TV

Cheese TV. Devastates me. Perfect family. Three.
Live with pain. Insane. Drain. Codeine-brain.

Dulled-high, magenta sky. Plagued fall, deathly pall.

Can't sleep. Can't eat. Certain defeat. When your young son
becomes the one you want to be like…

Cheese TV. Devastates me. Perfect family. Three.

In darkness awake. Alone but near. Utterly blighted. Entire
fear.
Place the pill upon your tongue my son and you'll be free. Lies.
Unbound knotted, spotted, smash-grab, brain-drab mendacity
for a mind-numb mass.
Release me. Free me. Let me float by in my own sky.
Not magenta-filled but busted with clouds, rooks, kites, night-
owls:
The fragmented creatures prowl.

But
But
But
How very real.
Kaleidoscopic real to be sailing free on a choppy-sea. Me.
Free to drown - a beautiful clown?

But free at last of pain-fuelled, drug-bound, haze-made,
magenta-plagued, locust-tongued, sky-bound but sea-found.
Drowned? They frowned.
Not the head-of-house, top-of-class clown?
Not drown?

Got down. Let down. Alone now. In space somehow. Believe
me. You three. You beautiful, wonderful three. The single
greatest things of me are you three. Do you see?

The sea, the earth, the stars, planets and galaxies, cannot create
the light in stilted night that beams so follow—spotted bright,
As is the blighted part of me that somehow went towards you
three.

I'm done. All undone. A walking mockery of hazy left-over
distant man-made star.
So bizarre. I haven't changed a bit. Not grown nor learnt one
thing.
Lost child, living his dream of cyclorama's magenta sky: fake
as slap.
Alone, but so unjustly loved, so heinously adored.

Pace around. Once boy-proud. Carved from some survival
mechanism a ritualised self-image of patient waiting.

Desperate. Ingratiating.

Cheese TV. Devastates me. Perfect family. Three.

Isn't it enough?

Isn't it enough that I could have been but wasn't?

Isn't it enough that I might have had but didn't?

Isn't it enough that I'm not enough even though I'm too much?

Isn't it enough that I spilt my drink, split my lip. Lost my way?

Isn't it enough that that day endures in me still, after all the surgery?

I'm still here. Shuddering. Alone in the night. Being defeated by blistering thoughts

That won't be still, that fidget like eels, that keep me blinking in the dark?

When is it enough?

When isn't it enough?

When there's nothing left to give.

No more schemes or dreams.

No more positivity.

Just inverted time. Like negative energy. Aligned to nothing.

To no one.

Nothing.

No.

What have I done to be tortured like this? To be wrenched and rendered incessantly? Without pause? Without cause?

What have I done that's so bad

That I'm made so incapably incapable?

So perfectly impossibly opposite?

Just

Just let me be
Just let me be free
Just let me be me
Just let me be
Just let me sleep
Just let me please, be…
This is killing what little life is left in me.
When light and sound conspire to make
The hour reject your bleeding pleading,
It's time to let it go, just let it all go,
Yes go.
Alone.
Now go.

Listen

It's good to do so yes of course,
But just listen to your body
Um… how do I do that?
Sense when you've had enough
And just listen to your body
No seriously HOW do I do that?
When you feel you've had enough
Just say, and rest. Listen to your body.

HOW do I do that? My body says go fast.
Get stressed. Don't sleep. Punish yourself.
Self harm. Selflessly unaware of what's best for me.

Seriously my body is the last thing I should be listening to. So,
I ask again.
What do I do to ride the waves of my incessant storm? What do
I do?
Just listen?

Tollund Man

Tollund Man
He does what he can,
Tollund Man!

Underneath

So, I'm underneath the rubber blanket again.
Crushing me.
My head is the rubber head again.
Chasing me.
My stomach flies about but nothing can come out. Or about.
I'm losing my way in this recovery….
Every day.
Every way.
I'm just hanging on, in there out of terror,
And love for my wife and kids.
I don't want them to go through the loss and pain and anguish
But…
But…
This rubber head sightless life is grinding, gnawing and
clawing.

How…how to get back?
How to be me again?
That's the daily mystery.
That's the daily misery.

Chapter 10
Eyesight Double-Vision Prism Lenses and Juggling!

One of the most challenging things to be left with in those early months of recovery was double vision (Terson's syndrome) and general lack of vision in my right eye. My right eye's retina had been ruptured by the aneurysm and my vision was clouded by blotches of blood. I was told that the aneurysm was in an inoperative place on the retina and would not heal. But, the professors at the eye hospital at John Radcliffe did reassure me that the brain would gradually compensate for the changes in my eyesight and that the double vision at least would eventually right itself to some extent. To what extent? However, this offered precious little comfort when my experience seemed to be that my vision was remaining the same, or even getting slightly worse. Everything from dog-walking to looking out of a car window would have roads and lines converging over each other and was profoundly disturbing and frustrating. Watching TV was impossible and I didn't really look at people making my daily existence quite isolating.

I decided that I needed to take some kind of action to attempt to retrain my eyesight. I thought that I needed to practice something that would improve my peripheral vision and try to force my eyes to straighten up. Really layman terms and probably completely inaccurate and ineffectual, but nevertheless I felt that I needed to try something to help: so, I thought of juggling! We learned to juggle at drama school, and over the years I've had intermittent stints at juggling. I had some juggling balls given to me by the drama students at City Lit as a 'thank you' for when I directed a graduation show there some years ago, so I figured if I could get to 100 juggles, I'd have to have reasonably good vision!

To begin with it was hopeless, just two or three juggles and the balls would crash to the floor, my hands flailing missing the balls by miles, our cocker spaniels Millie and Mabel barking excitedly around my legs trying to steal the fallen balls! Again! Try Again! Day after day! Hour after hour! Failure after failure!

But gradually though, ball after ball, drop after drop, failure after failure, I did start to improve. After a few weeks of trying, I got to my first 100 juggles! Yes! Was my eyesight any better? Not really! I guess perhaps my brain was adjusting making the juggling better with practice where my eyesight was the same. Still the same double vision.

It was then I learnt, from my ex-wife Claire (we remain great friends and always try to do the best for our kids. She has been incredibly supportive during this most challenging of times, and I am extremely grateful to her) of some research done in the States to help SAH survivors who typically had double vision issues: prism lenses that helped to retrain the muscle of the eye to see straight again. I googled prism lenses and saw that Specsavers offered them as part of their service! Amazing…I booked an appointment.

When the appointment came the optician was amazing. She looked into the right retina and could see the damage done by the aneurysm and said that as long as the double vision was in the main field of vision the prism lenses would work. I was lucky. As she tested differing lenses my vision was made more and more whole. Eventually she created the corrective prescription and ten days later I picked up my prism lens glasses.

The changes were gradual, but after wearing the glasses all day every day for two weeks or so I began to experience real progress. The double vision began to improve and after about a month of wearing the prism lenses my eyesight mostly had recovered. A miracle as far as I was concerned!

When I returned to the eye hospital for my check up six months post aneurism they were amazed. Not only was my vision completely fine, but unbelievably the retina was somehow healing itself. After much discussion the professors have concluded that the healing that has gone on in the retina may well be connected to T'ai Chi! The repetitive re-mapping of neural pathways may somehow have contributed to the healing of the retina. Writing this down sounds far-fetched, nevertheless I assure you this is the conversation that was held at my last appointment.

Amazingly then, my recent eye appointment appraisal states that my eyesight is back to normal and that I only need my prism lenses when tired. My big concern about ever driving again was answered directly where they state that my eyesight is now well above the threshold for driving competency. These days I juggle now and then, always 100 juggles plus! Just for fun!

Chapter 11
Horses

Being married to a show jumper it's inevitable that I'm very involved with horses. I first learned to ride when I was cast as Hareton Earnshaw in Wuthering Heights with Ralph Fiennes and Juliette Binoche. For six weeks or so before the shoot, I was picked up by one of the film's driver's Terry in his Jag and taken to horse stunt co-ordinator Steve Dent's farm for training. He put me straight onto his famous Lipizzaner stallion Chico. Steve's first words to me were: "Right, this horse has been in more films that you ever will, and he's worth a fortune so be careful with him. Don't let him turn to me when I'm in the menage with you because he's been taught to fight the whip and he'll rear!" I tried to give him a stroke and he bit me! Great start! Chico was indeed a very well-known stunt horse. Kevin Costner had just ridden him in 'Robin Hood Prince of Thieves' and the number of stuntmen that have told me since that they did their stuntman tests on Chico is incredible.

Anyway, within no time Steve had us cantering along centre lines, leaning over and picking up quoits as I went, get to a mark, get off in front of a practice camera, say a line, re-mount and canter off straight away, feet almost always out of the stirrups. It was amazing training three times a week for six weeks, and I'm eternally grateful to have been given the opportunity to learn on such an amazing horse. When Wuthering Heights was finished, I kept up my riding for a number of years, and being married to Faye of course I get to hack our horses (Heron and Qiko) out all the time to keep them fit.

Me riding Chico with Juliette Binoche

Heron

Heron is the most extraordinarily talented rising 10-year-old grade A show jumper. Faye and I bought him together when he was just an unbroken 3-year-old from Holland. He's the most sensitive boy, entirely connected to his 'wild' streak and to begin with he behaved in a very challenging way and can still have his moments! He loves his show-jumping and gets excited as soon as he hears the lorry starting up on show days. Faye and Heron have had huge successes over the years and were selected to represent the UK in the veterans European Championships in France, but were unable to go because I decided to have a brain aneurism at the time! Watching them jump is poetic and beautiful. Heron is so headstrong and fiery but Faye's gentle and sensitive riding coaxes the most amazing performances out of him. There's never a dull moment with 'Hezza' that's for sure!

Faye and Heron flying high and having fun!

Although I've ridden Heron from time to time, he's very sharp so since coming out of hospital I've been getting so much excellent rehab by riding (hacking out with Faye and Heron) on our youngster Qiko.

I've always had this connection with horses. And I guess partly because of my early riding training with Steve Dent, and just because it's how I am, I'm pretty much fearless when it comes to horses. I'm nothing compared to Faye as a rider, but she's the first to say what a good and brave horseman I am. I think that when you are riding fiery horses like ours anything you feel at all gets transmitted through the saddle and your legs to them. And they react. Therefore, you really do have to be quiet, calm and in-tune with them to ride safely.

When I first got back from hospital I struggled around the yard to Heron's stable. He's such a loving lad in spite of his fiery nature and would always lick me and play a game of taking my cap off my head in his teeth! Hold it for ages then gently drop it on the floor! Then demand hugs! I hadn't seen him for over a month and my hair still smelled of disinfectant from the shunt operation I'd had a few days before. I couldn't see straight and he must have been very aware of how sick I was because he turned to the back of his stable, before slowly coming back around and sniffing me. He was so lovely with me and it was such an emotional thing to see him again.

People who have animals in their lives will understand. When a horse loves you, it takes your breath away at times; their power and the choices they make to love us in spite of their extraordinary strength and instinct can be overwhelming. To have horses in my life as I struggled gingerly around the place in those first few weeks was so empowering and inspiring. But it was the moment when, after a schooling session with Qiko, that Faye said to me "put my helmet on and get on him and I'll just walk you to the stables" that my recovery really started to progress. I mean it was nothing more than being led in walk, but something about Qiko's heart and power and energy seemed to transfer to me and for the first time since coming out of hospital Faye saw me smile.

Qiko van het Lindehof

As a 4-year-old Qiko had really bad issues with his stifles. Lots of young horses have this and it presents as sticking or erratic movement from the stifle joint (kind of the elbow joint of the hind legs). The best remedy is actually exercise and strengthening by going to the water treadmill and by hacking up and down hills. By the time I went into hospital he'd had loads of treadmill treatment but obviously things were put on hold whilst I was away as Faye spent every spare minute visiting me at John Radcliffe. After a few weeks of being back home Faye knew exactly the right thing to say to me. I was feeling very sorry for myself, couldn't see very well at all and was very insular and introverted. "Qiko needs you to hack him out or he'll never get better. You can rehab each other!"

And with that, just a few days after sitting on Qiko and being walked from the school to the stables; we went for our first hack through the woods together. Faye on Heron, I followed on Qiko. And although I couldn't really see, although my body was weak and aching and although I was trembling with fear when I first got on him, after a few strides something happened. It was like his energy was going through me. I sat up straight and started to feel great. Although not as sharp as Heron, Qiko is still a fiery young boy, but somehow, we were able to crack on together in spite of everything. I genuinely believe that riding is like doing T'ai Chi. It connects me to Qiko's energy and power and heals me from within. I know this sounds crazy, and most people would think I'm mad taking such risks after four bouts of brain surgery.

But to me the risk of not riding is greater to my health and well-being. I recovered so quickly when riding. Faye said I was like a different person after that first hack. And I guess it makes sense. You have to transmit calmness and a sense of relaxed security to a horse like Qiko. You can't fake these feelings either! So in a way I've been forced to be fine when riding him. And that feeling of being fine has started to last. I mean I still struggle with brain fog and fatigue but physically I feel fully recovered, and for that I'm so very grateful to Faye and to our young horse Qiko. After all of our hacking, Qiko's got stronger and stronger and his stifle problem is now fixed. And he's doing incredibly well with Faye show jumping. What a lovely lad he is!

Back in the saddle! Qiko and me.

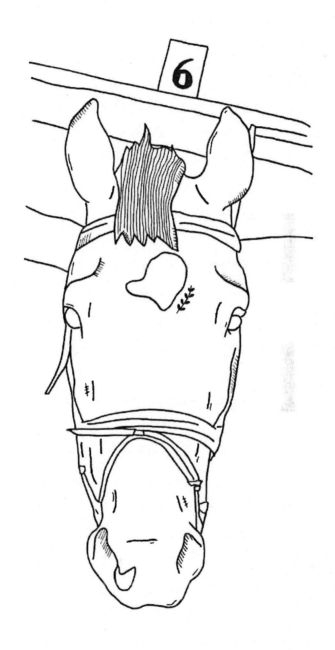

Chapter 12
Faye's Stories

June 29, 2021 Jason had been complaining of a headache for 3 days now and if I'm honest I just thought, like as he did that it was nothing serious. I was sat on the sofa after finishing work that evening when he came home still complaining of a terrible headache, as he walked into the hallway suddenly there was a horrible thud! Instinctively I knew exactly what had happened but for just a brief moment I wanted to pretend it hadn't. Jumping to my feet my worst fears were realised Jason had collapsed on the floor, I cried out to him whilst trying to wake him, he came around and started to speak so I up sat him against the wall. I grabbed my phone and called for an ambulance.

Jason said a few things giving his name and age to the guy on the phone then begun to start clenching his fists tightly whilst asking what was happening to him before falling over to his side and had what seemed a like a seizure, the emergency phone operator asked is he breathing and to be honest I couldn't stay calm enough to work that out, all I knew was he'd gone blue so by this point so I started CPR.

My God, it's a frightening place being stuck in a hallway with someone who is essentially dying and you can't call anyone for help other than a stranger. The first responder arrived and gave Jason an adrenaline shot; he regained consciousness but he was not cognitive. Soon, the air ambulance doctor arrived along with an ambulance and they spent the best part of an hour stabilising him before taking him to John Radcliffe. Mum and dad arrived to take the dogs and mum drove me to the hospital.

We were in times of Covid and I can empathise with anyone who had a loved one in hospital. When I arrived at the hospital, they confirmed it was a ruptured aneurysm and they thought there were 3 bleeds but they concluded it was just one and it was in a place where it could repaired. I was handed a phone in the reception to speak with the surgeon who would be taking care of Jason from here on in. He said they will operate to relieve the pressure by drilling a hole into his skull tonight and the following day they would do a procedure called coiling on the ruptured aneurysm. This operation has a low success rate and there's a high chance he will die but if we don't do it, he will die.

In normal situations I'd have sat with him all night but because of Covid I was sent home.

Jason spent the next day in surgery. After his operation I spoke with his surgeon who said the operation was successful however there can be many complications so don't get your hopes up! I was elated and obviously thought it's a smooth run from here on in. I think Jason and I both thought that so it was especially hard to cope with the tornadoes of shit that constantly came flying at us for the following month.

Post operation I called the nurse in ICU and he said Jason says he has a headache to which I thought was a joke! Totally an inappropriate one nonetheless but I fully expected him to be in a coma for a long period of time. I was totally shocked to find him chatting away and fully cognitive, he couldn't move his left foot fully but there was no stopping Jason he was back in the programme! I was so relieved I could hardly believe it!

Two days after the operation Jason was moved to the High Care Unit where he started to perk up more and things were looking great. He still had his brain drain attached to his head at this point and they discussed removing it the following day.

The brain drain was removed from his head. Jason's pain medication had stopped any bowel movements so he was given laxatives. Jason had become delirious at this point he was pretending to neigh and said he was Heron our horse!

The nurse reminded Jason he mustn't strain, in case the brain fluid leaked out his head, this went in one ear and out the other because before I knew it brain fluid was spirting out of his head like a fountain. The nurses rushed in and a few moments later Jason was wrapped up like a mummy! It all seems quite amusing now but at the time I was terrified.

The very next day Jason wasn't making any sense at all he believed there were evil nurses after him. His wonderful nurse James said we've tested his brain fluid and bloods, the bacteria markers coming back negative but I'm sure there is an infection. That evening they put him on antibiotics and we eventually discovered that he had bacterial meningitis.

Jason would always text me in the morning and I knew instinctively that this was the point in which Jason feels he almost died, he had a massive seizure that evening. The surgeon was so worried he never went home that night.

Everyone has a limit of how much they can handle and this point I think I'd reached mine. I stayed at Mum and Dad's and just lay on the sofa for the next 48 hours in-between visits. The only person I spoke to was a dear friend who had experienced her mum who'd had a serious brain injury which gave me huge comfort.

The very next day I woke up to find Jason was back on Facebook showing the world he was up able to walk around again.

The 2nd drain was put in his spine and it was there for what felt like a century. More than anything else this is what affected Jason the most mentally. If you move without assistance, you can literally kill yourself, the drain works on gravity so any wrong moves can cause a massive brain bleed. He was watched by the nurses 24/7 at this point they would sit on chairs and watch his every move.

Sometime later the drain was removed and he was due to come home the next day. I'd begun to notice Jason had no short-term memory! It was there and then it wasn't! He'd be on the phone all night and then he had no recollection of it! He had forgotten his daughter Emily had given birth and what her baby was called!

The only good thing about this was when Jason got recognised from his *Casualty* days, he asked me to print some photos of his that he could sign for them all. I thought to myself of course I can, in-between training 30 plus clients mucking out horses and travelling here every day, yes, I'm sure I've got time for that! I was actually thankful at that moment he'd forget in 5 minutes it ever happened!

By some stroke of luck in my hour visit I managed to catch the doctor who came around and said how is he? Jason as always said he was fine! (Translated— I might die in a few minutes) I interrupted and in my usual delicate manner I said, "Jason you can't remember your arse from your elbow you're not fine!"

The doctor concluded he would need to do another CT scan. We found Jason had hydrocephalus caused by the bleed that had blocked the capillaries so not allowing the flow of brain fluid; it was trapped building pressure which in turn gives dementia like symptoms. The plan was to do a series of lumber punctures in a last-ditch attempt to get the brain working correctly — if this didn't work they would need to insert a shunt to enable the fluid to drain from the brain into the stomach.

Jason came back to normal but unfortunately, he had to go ahead with the shunt operation.

Home

If anyone ever does anything useful in their lifetime learn first aid and always be aware of your blood pressure. That alone can save a life!

Jason came home and I was insistent of checking his blood pressure I was never told to but I'd been aware it was high in hospital. His was frighteningly high when he came home it was 178/128 when it should be 120/80, he is now on medication, and it's low again.

Recovery makes hospital seem like a holiday. The best way I can explain it is like you've both been thrown into the sea after a shipwreck and it's pitch black, you're treading water just praying someone will come to help you. It feels hopeless, every now and then you come up for air then you're pulled back down amongst the wreckage. There are no shortcuts or quick fixes it's a long arduous ride you venture on alone in your own world of pain. I don't know how anyone could ever do this without a partner because it's a very lonely place even when there are two of you.

I can guarantee anyone going through the same thing as a partner will feel relieved, lonely, angry, sad and bereft all at the same time. It's a multitude of emotions to deal with. No matter how much you don't want to believe it, your partner for this moment isn't the same and possibly will never be the same again. That may sound harsh but for a lot of couples in this situation you have to learn to love in some cases a totally different person.

Whilst I'm so lucky to have him here and I'm so thankful he is still Jason, I often find myself lost in a world of uncertainty wondering if he will ever get past the fatigue and enjoy our early mornings at the yard like we used to. This is just one of the little things I miss and all the things I do miss are little things, it's surprising to me how much the small things mean and we never really notice them until they are gone. Jason and I are two peas in a pod I can't think of a moment where we weren't by each other's side. The mornings on the yard are lonely without him, his brain fatigue has robbed us of those moments, he's no longer part of the coffee ritual and the horsey banter and I really miss that.

The truth is all the things I miss I try not to talk about with Jason because there is no one that wants them back more than him. He is suffering more than anyone and he is fighting an invisible battle. Jason at times believes he deserved this, his anxiety had been crippling and some days I don't know how we've made it through. In amongst all of this he still found the strength to learn something new because he wanted to help others. He qualified as a Personal Trainer so he could help rehabilitate others with fitness and T'ai Chi.

The braveness and determination, he has shown on a daily basis is astounding. It's true you never know what someone is going through not even those closest to you. All I know is I'm thankful he is here and that each day things get a little bit easier but you just can't rush recovery and as cliché as it sounds you have to be kind to yourself because this will test you to your limits.

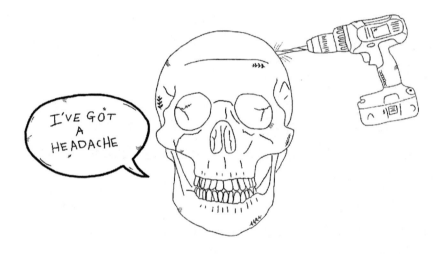

Chapter 13
Holiday—Getting Better

I think we know each other well enough now for me to be perfectly candid: I'm alive and speaking to you now because of my amazing wife Faye! How do my fellow brain injury survivors do it that are alone, or who don't have the undivided support of a loved-one, like my incredible Faye and my amazing family, the kids, Jean and Roger Faye's parents, and my mum Jackie and my brother Ryan? To say that you need help when in recovery from a brain injury is an understatement! It's an ongoing process of great success and crushing failure, normally when trying to do the most ordinary mundane things like going to the cinema (way too noisy, too much visual stimulation, too many people—I lasted 20 minutes!); or trips to the supermarket.

I think though, that we only get stronger by confronting the demons and finding a way through. To that end my Faye has an incredible instinct for what I need. Three weeks back from hospital she put me on our young horse Qiko and led me from the school to the stable like a donkey ride, and saw me smile for the first time since coming home. She just knew instinctively to do it. Her next instinctive choice to push the boundaries and get me better was to take me on holiday!

My birthday is in November and Faye thought it a brilliant idea for us to take a holiday to Tenerife as a present to me! She of course had been working every hour imaginable—she's a very successful personal trainer, but nonetheless having to work so hard to look after us both. Obviously, my earning potential went sideways, I'm still just learning how to do life in its simplest terms...again how do people do it without the support of a Faye in their lives? My experience has been that you fall in between every point of funding and support if you've made a great physical recovery like me.

Too well to qualify for support, not well enough to function to any great extent within broader society. I know MPs have been flagging the difficulties facing those of us with Acquired Brain Injury, but as of this moment we're in a pretty lonely place as far as any form of financial support is concerned. Medical support and the NHS on the other hand is phenomenal. I digress...

November put me over three months post my last brain surgery and eligible to fly: the amazing shunt operation on July 27, 2021 which regulates the fluid level in my brain was the last of four lots of major brain surgery. Amazingly, the shunt was invented by Roald Dahl who had a daughter who suffered from hydrocephalus and Roald Dahl lived in Great Missenden where Faye and I met and lived for a time!

The effect of hydrocephalus upon me was that I would have sudden on-set dementia and be unable to remember anything. I had numerous lumber-punctures in hospital in an attempt to remove the excess fluid, but my brain just couldn't handle it so the incredible surgery team at John Radcliffe intervened yet again, to insert a shunt into my brain to continually monitor and drain the excess fluid for me.

The shunt is basically a valve that takes excess fluid from the brain sack and it flows through a tube that passes down the inside of my neck, across my chest and into my tummy. All sounds a bit gruesome I know, and it took some time to get used to the odd feeling of a foreign object passing through me like that, but I'm cool with it now: it saves my life every day, how could I not be?

Panic about anything that might be wrong with you, a kind of clinical paranoia, grips me still and was very prevalent in my thinking back then. The idea of taking a flight filled me with terror. I had this dream that the shunt blew up like a balloon on the plane and I was writhing around the aisle in agony! Faye gave me pep talk after pep talk keeping me calm. Of course, when the day came everything was so easy. I passed through security and onto the plane without issue. The flight was wonderful! Success! An achievement to chalk up without a doubt!

The seven days we spent in Tenerife was idyllic. The sea, the sand, the pool, the food, the warmth on my skin was just what I needed. I took so much time to do T'ai Chi in as many memorable places as possible. On the shoreline, breathing in the clean sea-air, on the balcony of the room, by the pool…it was a great time of healing for me, both physically and spiritually. I think that break really helped me to begin to regain my confidence and for my strength to increase manifold. And for that I thank my beautiful, brilliant wife Faye, unreservedly. What would I do without her?

Chapter 14
Brain Gym! Taking My PT Qualification

The idea of taking a distance-learned qualification as part of my recovery filled me with dread and fear! Faye had always said that I should take my Personal Trainer qualification. In spite of my PGCE from my teaching days at Bedford Modern School, a PT qualification would certainly enable me to train people in T'ai Chi as a PT, a dream I've always had. After much persuasion that it would be good for me the day came that Faye bought me the qualification package from what turned out to be an amazing company Diverse Trainers. The day I opened on the computer the student support zone folder that 'housed' everything I needed to do to pass I wept uncontrollably! I could barely focus on the computer screen, let alone deal with the sheer volume of work to get through and the assessments to be taken. I was truly overwhelmed.

One of the tricky things about brain injury is that it seems to leave you with an inability to compartmentalise. You panic and get in a state of frozen terror that you will never again be able to achieve anything. Faye sat next to me and put my head in her hands, wiping the tears form my eyes, "You've got this, you can do it. Just focus on it a bit at a time. Little and often. You can do it!" And sure enough, bit by bit, assignment by assignment, I began to work my way through, passing theory module after theory module as I went.

I particularly enjoyed the zoom teaching sessions with the incredibly enthusiastic teachers. These live teaching experiences did me the power of good, and I made sure I asked as many questions as possible, again in a way I think I was forcing myself to do the things that actually filled me with fear. I decided not to tell the teachers at Diverse Trainers about my condition until I'd passed the course, it's therefore an amazing testament to Stephen, Ross, Chrissie and the team that they got me through it without realising the difficulties I was facing!

Their support for all of the students was amazing, and I'm so proud to say that after three months of solid hard work, having filmed training sessions with Faye and Phoebe at the local gym, my practical assessments went in and I passed the course! Wow! I did it! How cool is that! Whether you've had a brain injury or not, I thoroughly recommend stepping out of your comfort zone and learning something new.

THIS IS TO CERTIFY THAT

JASON RIDDINGTON-SMITH

HAS BEEN AWARDED

Focus Awards Level 3 Diploma
Practitioner in Personal Training (RQF)

This achievement included the successful completion of
the units detailed on the Unit Summary

QRN:	603/5233/4
Centre Name:	Diverse Trainers
Date Awarded:	10/11/21
Candidate Number:	JR031121
Certificate Number:	RQF33870

Chief Executive
Focus Awards

Chair
Focus Awards

ofqual
REGULATED
register.ofqual.gov.uk

Focus Awards, Silicon House, Farfield Park, Manvers, Rotherham, South Yorkshire, S63 5DB

0333 344 7388 I info@focusawards.org.uk

⊘ Verify authenticity at
www.focusawards.org.uk/verify

Chapter 15
T'ai Chi Qigong

Imagine this: you're standing on a beautiful grassy mound; all is greens and yellows as far as the eye can see. It's morning on a beautiful summer's day. The sunrise on the horizon makes the distant blades of grass and corn appear to shimmer and sway as a gentle morning breeze warmly caresses you. All is peace. As you breathe in deeply you can smell the sweet scent of summer in the air thick with lazy, hazy tranquillity. You gently breathe out, long and easy. Standing with your feet shoulder width apart and your knees slightly bent you go through your 'tension checklist': are your feet released and relaxed into the grass, are your knees tense and clenching or released and relaxed, are your hips free and relaxed, is the base of your spine released and relaxed, are you sucking your tongue to the roof of your mouth or is it released and relaxed in turn releasing tension in the throat, and are the back of the neck and shoulders released and relaxed? Yes? Good. Then let's begin...

Introduction

You 'open' the door to Qigong by gently lifting your straight arms away from your hips to the side until they raise to the top of your head and cross at the top to then flow downwards with palms straight down towards the ground, as you do this your knees bend whilst keeping heels and feet securely planted on the ground in parallel shoulder width apart. Back straight. You breathe in as the arms go up and out as they descend. This is repeated three times: slowly, as if moving through thick liquid.

Section 1: Chi

This section has the traditional Qigong exercises and is all about relaxation, gentle, graceful movements and breathing. The 'difficulty' level is simply governed by how deeply you bend the legs and how dynamic you make each move. Although each exercise repeats twelve times, you should think of each move as an individual entity trying to make the quality and dynamism of each movement as full and rich as possible. This is the meditative practice element of the form and is truly enlightening once you've been at it for a while.

Exercise 1

Standing in the same position feet shoulder width apart in parallel, gently lift your arms up to shoulder height and then back down with palms facing downwards. The movement should be slow and graceful as if moving through thick liquid, leading with the wrists; and paradoxically, see if you can visualise fire balls burning in your palms…feel the heat. This is your chi energy: your life force. As the arms descend bend the legs into as deep a bend as you can whilst keeping the feet planted flat on the ground, as the arms go up straighten the legs without clenching the knees. Breathe in as the arms go up and legs straighten and out as the arms descend and knees bend. Keep the back straight. Engage the core. Repeat this twelve times.

Exercise 2

This is the same as the first exercise except you cross your hands in front of you, right over the left, as they go upwards. Push down with palms facing the ground as before. And as before you breathe in as you go up, out as you go down, knees gently straightening and bending as you flow up and down breathing in and out. Slowly and elegantly as if flowing in thick liquid. Repeat twelve times. Engage the core. Visualise fireballs in the palms of your hands.

Exercise 3

The feet and legs remain the same here as in the previous exercise. The arms start with the palms of the hands resting on the thighs. Bend the knees fully back straight at the start. As you breath in raise the arms together, wrist first, slowly as if in thick liquid. At shoulder height turn the palms to face each other and take the arms out wide, palms facing out front. The knees are straight but not clenched. At this point the breath is fully inhaled. Now exhale and reverse the move by taking the hands to the front of the chest facing each other, and then down to the thighs again, breathing out and bending the knees. Repeat this twelve times.

Exercise 4

Still facing straight ahead pick up the right foot and gracefully lunge to the right, feet still in parallel. As you do this lift your right arm in a 'c' shape over your head and allow the left hand to flow out from the chest palm facing upwards, breathe out as you do this, then reverse the movement onto the other side and breathe in. Flow as if being blown on a gentle breeze, but paradoxically with a quality of thick liquid. Visualise and feel the fireballs in the palms of your hand. Breathe in one way and out the other. Repeat twelve times on each side.

Exercise 5

Feet still in parallel shoulder width apart bring both arms up around you as if you were doing the butterfly stroke in swimming. As your arms go upwards and to the side bend your knees and then straighten them so that the knees are straight but not clenched at the apex of the 'swimming stroke'. Breathe in as the arms get to the top then breathe out and bend the knees again as the hands trace downwards, palms facing the floor. If you imagine doing the butterfly stroke but standing up as you do it you've got it! Slowly like in thick liquid. Repeat twelve times breathing in as you get to the top of the stroke and out as you descend again in a circular motion.

Exercise 6

Standing with feet in parallel shoulder width apart, bend the knees as deep as you can go whilst keeping your feet flat on the floor. Keep your back straight and engage the core. Put your palms facing each other about six inches apart and see if you can feel the heat between your palms. This is your chi; it's really starting to flow in you now. Can you feel it? Next, take a comfortable step forward on your right foot and allow the left foot to twist slightly so that the toes face outwards and to the left. Knees bent in an 'en garde' position. Next, with your palms facing outwards away from you, put your hands up to your armpits as if you were about to push something away from you.

Imagining the fireballs in both hands and keeping the elbows facing outwards at shoulder height, push and bend the right knee hands going outwards as if pushing against something. Don't bend the back forward and be sure to keep the hips from breaking backward. Breathe out as you push forward then, when you reach the end of the push in full lunge forward, bend the left leg and straighten the right as you pull backward to the original position, breathing in. Repeat this twelve times then change to the left leg in front and repeat twelve times.

Exercise 7

This is exactly the same as exercise five except when you lunge forward the arms make a circular motion at shoulder height without crossing the hands in front. As you pull back bend the supporting leg in a 'defensive' lunge hands coming into the chest. Repeat breathing out as you go forward and in as you go back. Begin with the right leg forward in 'en garde' then change to the left leg forward. Repeat twelve times on each side.

Exercise 8

Standing with feet in parallel shoulder width apart bend the knees as deep as you can go whilst keeping the feet flat on the floor. Keep your back straight and engage the core. Put your palms facing each other about six inches apart and see if you can feel the heat between your palms. It's your chi. Can you feel it?

Take your right hand and put it up to shoulder height facing away from you as if you were about to push the fireball from you. Take your left hand and put it against your left hip palm facing downwards. Push the right hand away from you until the arms is fully extended but not locked breathing out as you do this. Then turn the right hand so that the palm is facing you bringing it slowly towards you slightly. Bring the left hand up to the right and kind of scoop out of it the fireball, breathe in as you 'take' the chi then place the left hand palm outwards against the left shoulder, right hand to right hip palm facing downwards and repeat. Breathe out as you extend and push the fireball away from you and breathe in as you take the fire from one plan to the other. Repeat twelve times on each side right then left: One, one, two, two, three, three etc…

Exercise 9

Exactly the same as exercise eight except you scoop the fireball from behind you like a front crawl motion and then exchange the fire as the hands pass in front of you. Breathe in as you collect the fire from behind and breathe out as you push the palm away from you. Twelve times on each side, one side after the other. Keep the knees bent and soft, engage the core and keep the back straight. Check no tension has crept in and that you aren't sucking the tongue to the roof of the mouth. Relax. Slow graceful movements.

Exercise 10

Feet in parallel knees bent. Put your left arm up to face height, looking at your palm, bent at the elbow, all at eye level. Your right hand is at your right hip, held open and facing the ground, elbow bent slightly. Twist the body to the left as far as the torso can twist, keeping the knees bent, breathing out. When you reach the end of the twist, change arms putting the right in front of the face, left to the hip palm facing the floor and follow the elbow all the way around to the right breathing in. Repeat twelve times. One, one, two, two etc…Visualise the fire balls in the palms of both hands here.

Exercise 11

Imagine standing in the centre of an empty room and see the corners diagonally in front of you. Bend the legs. Breathe out and lift the right hand up, palm facing upwards as if scooping a fireball upwards, tracing the diagonal line to the left. As the right arm comes down, exchange the fireball with the left hand and trace the right diagonal of the 'room', breathe in as you do this. Allow the legs to rise and fall, straighten and bend, as the arms go up and down. Twelve repetitions on each side. One, one, two, two etc...

Exercise 12

This time we're going to trace the diagonal lines in the room behind us, with both arms. Bend the legs, feet in parallel, and breathe out taking both arms behind us to the left straightening the legs as we get to the apex; then breathe in and trace the line to the opposite corner behind you. Straighten the legs as you get to the top of each corner, bend as you return to the centre. Visualise fireballs in the palms of your hand.

Exercise 13

Feet still in parallel shoulder width apart legs bent but feet flat on the floor. This exercise is flying. Picture yourself as a giant eagle you extend your giant wings elbows leading lifting up straightening your legs as you breathe in, then breathe out as you 'flap' your wings down to your sides, palms facing the ground. Breathe out and bend your legs as you do this. Repeat twelve times. Keep your back straight but allow the head and neck to flow freely up and down with the motion and you fly.

Exercise 14

Now standing feet slightly wider than shoulder width, knees straight but not locked, just drop the head gently down towards the left knee, breathing out and tracing the shin with your hands to the left foot. Come back up breathing in and then repeat this on the right side breathing out. These are just a little leg stretch in preparation for the next exercise.

Exercise 15

This exercise is a 'salutation to the sun'. Standing legs straight feet slightly wider than shoulder width, lift the left toes to point up and out so that you are resting on the heel, bend the right knee. Holding this position take both hands down to the left shin, head towards the knees breathing out, then breathing in come up and raise your hands above your head (hands up!) as if you are welcoming the sun. Repeat this twelve times to the left and then twelve times to the right. Breathe out as you go down and in as you go up.

Exercise 16

Full lunge to the left, back straight allowing the right foot to pivot forming an L shape from left foot to right. Keep the right leg straight as you bend the left in full lunge to stretch out the adductor muscles. Hands can rest on the left knee. Repeat on the left. This exercise is in preparation for the next exercise.

Exercise 17

Still in lunge face the front and imagining a pane of glass just in front of you. With palms face out wipe the pane of glass in a circular motion as you lunge from the left to the right. Breathe out to the left and in to the right. Repeat twelve times then pause and reverse the exercise going to the right first. Repeat twelve times.

Exercise 18

Feet back in parallel knees bent, back straight. Hand relaxed down by your thighs facing you. Imagine there is string attached from your middle finger to each knee. Breathe in and pick up the right knee with the hand by gracefully lifting the hand up to head height and then back down gently replacing the foot. This should be slow and graceful and well balanced. Repeat twelve times alternately on each side. One, one, two, two etc…

Section 2:
Stretch

Exercise 1

Stand in a star shape: legs slightly wider than shoulder width apart, straight but not clenched. Straight back, arms in a V shape above your head straight out with palms facing outwards. Imagine a beam of white light coming from your palms and encircling the globe with you at the centre point.

Pull up and out to the right-hand side stretching the left side upwards. Keep the body perfectly square. Breathe in then breathe out holding for a count of twelve.

Lean over further to the right into a full side bend, stretching the left side. Breathe in then out for a count of twelve.

Allow the head to relax down to the right knee, hands down to the right foot. Don't force anything just feel the stretch in the hamstring of the right leg and the spine and neck. Breathe in then out as you hold for a count of twelve.

Take your head into the middle in between the legs. Just relax and allow the weight of the head and torso to stretch the hamstrings. Stay comfortable, putting the hands around the ankles if you can. Breathe in then out holding for a count of twelve.

Next go to the left, putting the head towards the left knee. Breathe in then breathe out and hold for a count of twelve.Next go to the full stretch with arms out high above the head to the left side. Breathe in then breathe out and hold for a count of twelve.

Then pull upwards to the left, breathe in and out for a count of twelve.

Then do a full plié bending the legs as deep as you can with the heels on the floor and the back straight. Allow the arms to go downwards in a circular motion with the palms facing downwards. Breathe out. Then reverse and take the arms back up to the original V shape breathing in.

Now do the whole thing again but going to the right first. Repeat the entire set eight times, gently increasing the stretch and the dynamics of each move as you go.

Exercise 2

Full deep lunge to the left, arms outstretched to the side, right leg straight, right foot planted in an L shape to give strength and balance. Breathe in then breathe out for a count of twelve as you stretch.

Breathe in coming to the centre with both legs in a deep bend. Back straight. Arms upwards above the head but palms facing each other.

Then get into a deeper bend with the hands facing upwards against the hips, thumbs tucked in. Breathe out.

Then repeat the deep lunge to the right as before. After this, repeat the whole thing four times, alternating on each side. Don't push it too much but try to increase the stretch each time.

Exercise 3

Next comes another set of full lunges but this time when you lunge to the left place the hands palms down on the floor in front of the left leg that you're lunging on. Breathe in, then breathe out straightening the left leg allowing the head to fall downwards towards the left knee. Repeat four times on the left side, then four times to the right getting the head further towards the knee each time without straining.

Exercise 4

Stand up straight feet shoulder width apart hands to the sides. Breathe in, then breathing out roll the head downwards to the knees being the legs. Hold onto the back of your calves or your ankles, breathe deeply into the small of the back. Breathe out as you straighten the legs, allowing the head to be guided towards the knees but do not strain. Breathe out. Bend the knees and breathe in; straighten and breathe out. Repeat four times. On the fifth time when the knees bend roll the torso back up to standing. Then repeat the entire exercise, bending and stretching the legs with the head to knees four times. The breathing is very important. Breathe out when you stretch and breathe in when you release.

Section 3:
Strength

Exercise 1

Standing with feet shoulder width apart. Back straight. Bend the knees and hold the arms out at shoulder height as if you were holding a barrel. Breathe deeply. Hold this pose for a count of 100 if possible, or whatever count you are comfortable with.

Exercise 2

Next take a step outward to the right with your right foot. Feet still in parallel. This time imagining holding the base of barrel down low. It's rising on your thighs as your legs bend as deep as you can. Breathe deeply. Hold for a count of 100 or as long as you feel comfortable.

Exercise 3

Next take a big step out to the right and push your hands out to the sides as if you were Samson pushing the column apart. Visualise a beam of light coming from one palm encircling the earth and going into the other palm. Deep plié (bend) with straight back. The deeper you bend the harder it is. Hold for a count of 100 or to whatever is comfortable.

Exercise 4

Next lean to the left and hold the arms with palms facing up as if holding up two vases at head height. Place the calf of the right leg onto the bent knee of the left and balance. Keep breathing and hold for a count of 50 or as long as is comfortable.

Exercise 5

Gracefully place the right leg back into the full bend position with the arms pushing out to the side. Hold for a count of 100 if you can. Breathe deeply. Try to relax even though it's hard.

Exercise 6

Next lean to the right and get into the same pose balancing with the left leg crossed over the right, holding the imaginary vases up. Keep breathing and hold for 50 if you can.

Exercise 7

Now go back to the deep bend with arms using out to the sides for a final count of 100 if you can.

Exercise 8

Now take a step, inwards with the right foot going back to the low pose holding the imaginary barrel on your thighs. Keep breathing and hold for a count of 100 or whatever is comfortable.

Exercise 9

Take a further step to the right, still with bent knees going back to the original barrel hold at shoulder height. Keep breathing deeply and hold for a count of 100 or whatever you're comfortable with.

Conclusion

We end our T'ai Chi Qigong session together by closing the chi door. Stand feet shoulder width apart knees slightly bent. Raising the arms above our heads in a circular motion away from our sides palms facing upwards we breathe in, then we push downwards to the ground palms facing downwards breathing out and bending the knees. Repeat this three times.

Meditation

After the 'conclusion' movements place the left hand on the abdomen, right hand over the left. Put the knees together and bend slightly and bow the head slightly. Close your eyes. Imagine that you are now storing all of that chi energy, locking it into your T'ai Chi box. Go through the tension checklist ensuring relaxation of feet, ankles, knees, hips, small of the back, neck and shoulders and tongue. Breathe into the hands and small of the back.

Visualise going through the first section of Qigong again but imagine yourself on a grassy mound, looking out onto a beautiful horizon beyond. As you go through each exercise in your mind picture real fire burning in the palms of your hands, flickering and smacking as you move. Keep this visualisation going until the end of section 1 or as long as you can gradually increasing the time until you can do all of section 1 in your mind…open your eyes.

Chapter 16
Me

1.

I've titled this chapter 'Me' but it could just as easily be called 'You' or 'Us' because it encompasses some empirical truths that underly all of our existences whether we're aware of them or not. The archetype of our collective existence is what we experience and process as reality: as truth. And what makes **me** so aware of this 'truth' I hear you ask? What makes me so big-headed or arrogant as to believe I have answers to questions such as the nature of what is true for us sentient beings? Well, let me just say that near death experiences bring to the surface an ancient life-force that puts you in touch with the stark truth of nature's power to create and to destroy; and that you become very aware of your own small place within the spectrum of creation and destruction: life and death. This awareness makes you live each moment more fully than before. This is hard to explain…To do this part of my story justice we'll need to go back in time some thirty years or so.

I first met the actor, explorer and author Brian Blessed some thirty years or so ago. We were doing a play together, 'The Lion in Winter' at the rep theatre in Colchester. He was playing the irascible King Henry and I was playing one of his children, the conniving Geoffrey. Immediately I felt like I had 'come home' in his presence. You're probably thinking of him as the loud, bombastic persona so many know and love him for, but I, like his good friend the Dalai Lama, know him as one of the quietest most profound souls upon the planet. I could tell you so many incredible stories about Brian! But that's not what this book is about. Suffice it to say that one day, in my hospital bed I received a voicemail from my old friend, none of which is repeatable here! But it was distributed to the surgery team so wonderfully hysterically and profoundly moving were his messages of support for me and all at John Radcliffe hospital.

Since then, Brian has continued to call me every couple of weeks to get an update on my progress. On one of these phone calls, after I'd been out of hospital some three weeks or so, I tearfully told him how close to the edge I was. How I couldn't sleep. How I was so tortured by the Crow-man's nightly visits. And this, roughly speaking, is what he told me: "You have tasted death Jason. This puts you at a massive advantage in life. You can help so many people in the future because tasting death gives you power.

"Your consciousness has become in touch with the ancient reptilian part of the brain, we're doing research but know virtually nothing about the brain. Indeed, there are more synapses and connections in the human brain that are unexplored than there are planets in the cosmos. You must understand that this experience is a gift for you. The reptilian part of the brain is where ancient hunter gatherer man resides. You have become aware of the presence of death, and your crow-man keeps you focused upon this not to frighten you but to help you survive.

"Think of it this way. You are now like our ancient ancestors, aware of the dangers that lurk behind bushes. Modern man has no idea and would wonder along and be eaten within five minutes by the creatures that lie in wait for us all.

137

You've become attuned like one of your fantastic sensitive horses that can sense danger before anything happens. And that's all it is. Nothing more. You're not in any danger it's passed. You've beaten it. You're getting better. But you have to accept that you have become a different being: a better being: a more in tune being. This process will empower you and enrich you. You have nothing to fear…"

You see why this man is so special to me? And by the way he's the reason you're reading this book— "You must write the book…If you don't finish the book, I'll knock you into next week! You tell everyone that's what Brian Blessed said!"

This notion of the reptilian ancient part of the brain has also been explored with me by the excellent psychologists with whom I've been having support sessions. And thinking about it, it makes total sense. I believe treatment for PTSD due to near-death experiences is actually more like prizing us back from that ancient fight or flight modality that is mainly nullified in today's artificially 'safe' but complex world. It sounds like I'm promoting the reptilian brain and in many ways I am. Having come back from the brink I can honestly say that there's loads and loads of stuff about the way we live today, as I've struggled to fit back into society, that I find wholly at odds with what I've learned about the indomitable nature of the human spirit.

Imagine for a minute a herd of flight animals, sheep for example. Now flight animals survive not by running from preying animals, often then it's too late, but by anticipating dangers that most of the time do not actually exist. These imagined dangers are triggered by other members of the herd reacting to noises or the presence of something that mostly isn't there. Sometimes the threat is real though, that's what makes the reaction so intense throughout the herd. The imagined threat is as real as the real thing. If you were to ask sheep number #2 why he ran, he'd say because number #1 did, and number #1 would say he thought he heard number #23 say there was something over there etc etc! Such is the way of sheep.

But we are not sheep. We are not flight animals. We are hunter gatherers. In our native state and at the height of our natural powers we are aware of danger, acutely aware, but we are not afraid of it. We strategise how to master the danger, how to beat it. We calculate and plan and create and nurture and care for those we love. But we cannot do this if we are out of tune with the hunter gatherer, if we are afraid, if we are sheep.

2.

Many thousands of years ago you were a little girl called Ra. You lived with your parents and your older brother in a small village on the edge of a vast and mighty forest. Your people settled in this clearing in the summer months, moving into treehouses in the forest in the winter. The world was warmer then, and the air was thick and sweet with the smells of abundant nature. The villagers would hunt and forage and kept horses. Your father's horse Hadad, which translated into modern English means Thunder was a sleek black stallion. Still half wild he only allowed father to ride him.

One day many of the villagers, including father and Thunder went off to hunt and to forage. You were left happily playing in the tall grasses as you watched the hunting party disappear into the distance. Then you heard a snap and a snort. A thud of a heavy snout upon the low-lying branch of birch tree. Silence. You froze in fear: desperately listening for the next sound to get some sense of where the threat was coming from. Behind you, heavy breathing; you turned to see Balak, the most feared of all of the wild boar of the forest. Six feet tall he stood prone, his old tusks curling around the snarling snout all drenched with sweat and saliva. You were rigid with fear, Balak! The children's songs were right. He was the devil from the forest. The beast that brought death and destruction. He stared deep into your eyes, into your soul. Your heart raced, as tears of panic flooded your cheeks.

Suddenly from behind you the sound of hooves on the earth and a flash of gleaming black as father and Thunder charged between you and Balak. Father turned the great stallion to face you and as he did his powerful hind legs flashed out in rage at the side of the charging boar, catching him square in the ribs, sending him into the air. Father then turned the brave stallion towards the raging Balak and before he had a chance to get back on his feet and attack, father leapt from the horse's back, plunging his glinting knife deep into the boar's chest. Balak frantically kicked out but father drove the knife deeper and deeper until finally the devil from the forest lay lifeless. Thunder pranced and neighed and blew his nostrils in triumph as father, all blood and sweat ran to your side to check you weren't hurt.

That night you gave Thunder such a hug as he stood all sleepy in his paddock. A great fire was burning in the centre of the village, sending jets of orange and red into the star-filled sky. The villagers sang songs around the fire and laughed and told their stories of father and Thunder, of the little girl named Ra and of Balak the devil from the forest. Everyone ate and drank and went off to a sound and happy sleep. Enough to eat, warmth and safety were the daily ambitions of your little society, your beautifully simple community. As you lay there that night, next to the smouldering fire, you could hear the deep breathing of Thunder in his field and you smiled as you watched a star shoot across the night sky. What a day! And what a horse! And with that you drifted off to sleep.

3.

Sometimes contentment can seem to be very illusive and can seem to be dependent upon so much more than was the case for our ancestors. But is it true? Is life really so much more complex? Do we really require so much more from our lives than warmth, food and nurturing?

You don't have to be a Buddhist or believe in reincarnation to be able to see yourself as Ra. In fact, this ability to imagine ourselves in another's situation, to feel their pain, hope, anguish, fear, love and so on is one of the things that makes the human condition so unique within the animal kingdom. Empathy with others is the genesis of catharsis that was experienced by ancient Greek audiences watching their epic tragedies and is the 'magic if' referred to by Stanislavsky when an actor builds a character in his 'method' books. Visualising scenarios is the 'what if' processes 'running' the possible fight or flight scenarios in the mind when we evoke potential situations that might befall us.

If we are honest these fear-based processes are pretty much a permanent fixture in our minds. We are always in an internal state of fight or flight as a result of the inner dialogue, the constant diatribe of scenarios that almost never come true. Mostly we live in a constant state of fear, discontentment and dissatisfaction with ourselves and our current realities. Nothing is ever enough, hence the constant voices and scenarios, eternally playing out, running like a noisy generator in the background of our thinking.

The dubious luxury of 'what if' thinking is something that I've found very problematic post SAH. Brain injury makes **all** thinking and doing hard, let alone the multi-layered problem/scenario thinking that we tend to indulge in all of the time. And having a brain injury to recover from with the attendant pains and aches and insomnia makes for fertile ground for worried thinking that can take over a good mood and destroy.

I'm not suggesting that we can control our 'what if' tendencies, in fact I think it's something that we all do automatically all of the time. In that sense then, we are out of control. But I do believe we can change what it is we focus upon. I definitely think that keeping things simple and living in the moment is sound advice for those of us recovering from brain injury, I also believe there are teachings from our ancestral collective psyches that, when contrasted with the modern experience, can be enlightening: like the story of Ra.

Basically, having brain injury is like living with a shrunken capacity for what I can engage with before I overflow and lose it emotionally. And it's like I can feel my brain, churning, turning, being heavy… When that happens, everything becomes desperate and despairing. I'm unable to feel like things are ok, moreover it feels like panic and desperation are the only reality that I'll ever experience. But there is a way back. When I'm doing T'ai Chi it's like I'm doing, living, breathing recovery. When I'm riding Qiko, although he's fiery and young I'm in the moment with him, at one with him and I'm free. But what of the rest of the time? How can I feel ok? Maybe I need to be really selective about what I put into my brain? Maybe I need to be careful? I think the story of Ra is important for us brain injury sufferers. The fact that for millennia the human species lived free of virtually all of the things that modern day humans get so concerned about is important.

Ra had her family and immediate community to care about. If she did worry about the good opinions of others, she was limited to the immediacy of the people she actually knew and lived with. With us it's so very different. Our 'what-if' way of thinking is able to run rampant when given anonymous social media 'likes-fear' to feed upon incessantly. We continually engage the 'other' part of us: the part of us that should be empathising with our fellow travellers is actually mostly living within the unreality of our 'smart' devices that take us away from our natural state of awareness and make us behave like sheep.

Hunter gatherers do not live in fear, we should live in alert awareness: but not fear. The modern experience has created an environment fraught with psychological danger for those of us trying to recover from brain injury. All around us, everywhere, are constant invitations to disappear down the rabbit hole of fear and self-loathing. We worry globally without taking care of the small details at home at our peril. We become victims of victims. Dependent upon pleasing 'them' we drown in a sea of platitudes unable to fully grasp the world again that we so nearly lost: so, we opt out.

My experience is that opting out of much that modern life offers is actually the sensible option for those of us recovering from brain injury. Here are a few ideas I've had of things to be avoided, changed or just plain boycotted:

- Limit time spent on social media.
- Do not post on social media if getting 'likes' becomes important.
- Spend time in nature.
- Spend time with animals.
- Focus your attention on immediate friends and family.
- Don't worry about what you can't do. Focus on what you can do.
- Learn something new, but avoid failure.
- Try doing T'ai Chi.
- Keep good company be that music or friends.
- Make each day count for something, no matter how small.
- Don't worry about not being able to sleep. Do some writing, listen to music or read a book, don't go on your phone…you will sleep.

It's very easy to feel useless. I know I do a lot of the time. The future can seem daunting. Just writing these words I'm aware of my changed way of thinking and how draining that thinking is. It's hard to express myself, the words just aren't there in the way they were before. It's tough. And it's a disability that is invisible to most other people. You look normal but feel so very abnormal and out of touch. Learning to reintegrate into society following brain injury is a lengthy process insomuch as the brain itself seems to have its own repair time-scale that will always trip you up when you thought you were fine.

Learning when to stop is very important. As is taking power naps and rests when the red mist descends and you get stuck. I've had some pretty embarrassing 'brain-stuck' moments! Like the time I went to Lidl to buy a few things and the isles to me became two-dimensional and I literally got stuck. I had to walk out of there agonising step by agonising step, holding onto the walls as I went. I must have looked mad, or drunk or something! When I got home came the tears of profound self-loathing, "I can't even do that!" It's so very tough. But then you see the funny side of things, "I got stuck in the middle of Lidl!" It becomes a story that can actually help others and therefore has value no matter how dreadful it felt at the time. Learning to laugh is a useful way to put things into their true perspective. Give yourself a break and be happy with what you have achieved, be happy with the stuff you can do.

Learning to lower my expectations has actually meant learning to change the things I truly value. I think I've spent most of my life being very driven, which actually inculcates a sense of discontentment and irritability with where I'm 'at'. Brain injury forces you to stop, pause and to re-assess the things you truly value in life.

Sometimes I question why I'm still here. I mean what was the point in fighting so hard for survival if my life now is so difficult to live successfully. I mean I'm told all the time how well I'm doing and what a miracle I am, but at the end of the day those well-meant comments don't give me an income or a career. I can only be **so** good at something and then the fatigue hits me so it's like I'm consigned to a life of enforced mediocrity. Ambition seems pointless, trying hard just exhausts me. So, here's the question again: what's the point in me?

I'm gradually learning that the answer to that question is very dependent upon the day the question is being asked. At the time of writing, I'm eight months in. Eight months ago I had my SAH and my seizure and all the hell that went with it, and at this point in time I feel like I'm several different people in one body: I'm completely ok, full of energy and positivity; I'm dedicated to T'ai Chi and to sharing the power of T'ai Chi with fellow brain injury sufferers in the world; I'm full of energy and focus riding horses and doing T'ai Chi, I'm very in touch with my physicality but my mind is like a gyro I can't shut down at night...so I write; I'm unable to sleep; I'm unable to get up in the mornings, when I do get up my body aches and my head aches as I struggle to make my first coffee and take my anti-seizure, anti-depressant, blood-pressure and pain killer medication, I feel like shit and it'll take at least an hour to get going... These are some of the many versions of me.

Often, I'm stuck, full of fear and loathing for myself. I can't move and can't see a way out of these feelings. And the feelings are brought upon me by outside forces. Having a brain injury to fight through each morning is like having an invisible person standing in front of you repeatedly punching you in the face. You are not responsible for the fact you're being hit. But all anyone else sees is your reactions to the ongoing (but invisible to them) attack, and they focus their attention on your behaviour, your mood or your mind-set without really comprehending that you're not moody, or depressed: you're actually just fighting. Fighting a fight not of your choosing; and fighting a fight not of your making; but nevertheless, you ARE having to fight.

As unpalatable as it may seem to our modern sensibilities, sometimes standing up and fighting the invisible foe that is manifest with brain injury **is** the best option. It really can sometimes be the **only** option. It's my contention therefore that we brain injury survivors need to be as in-tune as we possibly can be with the reptilian ancient part of the brain in which resides our ancestral fight mechanism. Become aware of the fight. Be furious you are in this fight if it makes you feel better, but ultimately you need to accept that the conflict is there. It is real. And you need to get your game-face on and fight, fight, fight.

The challenging thing here is that you can feel like you are on your own with this fight. You think no-one, except other brain-injury survivors, knows what it is to suffer in this way and no-one can ever understand what a monumental fight you have to stoically face every day just to get to point zero. Getting up. Getting out. Getting to work. Getting things done. All of these normal everyday things to do requires fierce fighting for in order to be able to get them done.

It's a heart-breaking truth, but I'm just not as good at doing things as I was before: I struggle in crowds. I struggle with noise. I struggle with too much light. I struggle knowing where to look. If I'm to speak I hear myself echoing in my mind like I'm in a cave. If I'm asked a question I pause and stammer and struggle to form my words. When I'm left alone, I'm either having to sleep to recover myself, my brain feeling like a lead weight in my head; or I'm wired like a junkie unable to shut down at all. I have never spent so much time on my own as I have since my brain injury and I'm with Faye all the time! What must life be like for my fellow brain injury survivors who don't have a Wonder Woman like my Faye in their lives? I'm so lucky…

I guess all I'm saying here is that the insomnia time alone, the changed thought processes and the inherent and subsequent lack of confidence speaks volumes for how much brain injury actually takes us away from others into realms that we'd rather not be in. But, we are very much in those realms.

Therefore, my fellow travellers I advise T'ai Chi, or something similar.

That said though I do recognise that I'm one of the lucky ones. I really did come out of this pretty well unscathed, as hard as the recovery has been and continues to be.

4.

So, what are the things that I've learned from this experience that I might share with you? Well, my friend, whether you're in recovery from a brain injury or not, I reckon there are things that can unite and unify us in physical, mental and spiritual recovery and care for each other. In the 21st Century physical conflict with each other should be a thing of the past. The nuclear stakes are simply too high for us to toy with bashing each other anymore. We are a global community and as such all of us are brothers and sisters. We need therefore to manage our ancestral fight or flight instincts and to recognise the benefits of the ancient reptilian brain, without engaging with or entertaining our fear-laden aggression and prejudices. Alert awareness makes me useful to others; self-obsessed paranoia makes me useless.

In a sense T'ai Chi is like a constant form of teaching. Tasting the limitless power whilst practicing T'ai Chi makes me aware of how far away from my potential I remain for most of the day. My thinking wavers and jumps like a butterfly from one worry to another, and yet when in the flow of T'ai Chi the limited becomes so limitless. All is potential in the sublime stillness attainable when chi courses through your veins: life and beauty, power and love. I'm not suggesting that T'ai Chi is the only way, far from it. But I do think that we need some form of meditative practice to keep us walking in the light and to keep at bay the dark forces that can overwhelm any one of us at any time.

My brain injury has forced me to stop and to reassess the fabric of my existence, of life itself. In the dark days of the

Ukrainian crisis, we all perhaps have considered our own mortality a little more lucidly than before. Certainly, coming face-to-face with death as I have, I appreciate life all the more; even if what used to be my dubious status quo now incurs in me as inner conflict and external struggle to keep afloat in the post SAH storms that rage incessantly. I remember reading once, 'you can't stop the waves but you can learn to surf' and I guess that's ultimately what this book is about. I'm just exploring ways in which we can all help each other to surf the inevitable waves of life a little better. Brain injury makes the storms that rage more obvious than before, the storms were always there though, just beneath the surface.

Maybe this is a blessing? Maybe **having** to become more peaceful, more self-aware, more 'chi' is a gift from the universe? Perhaps…I can't really remember now what I was like before. I guess I've become the adapted version of me. Or perhaps that's just what we're all doing all of the time? Continually adapting and evolving? What's important is to have some say, some hand in how you adapt and evolve: we can't change the circumstances of life, but we can choose how we react to those circumstances. To that end I truly believe that a meditative, spiritual practice like T'ai Chi enables and allows the better parts of us to flow freely. Fear cripples us in every sense, T'ai Chi and other meditative practices liberate us.

The ancient life-force that inhabits the reptilian brain is released, freed to dance gloriously in light and love with control and grace when we engage in spiritual practices like T'ai Chi and meditation. In spite of the many tendencies to the contrary we **do** have the capacity to find stillness, holiness and nirvana in the everyday, whether in recovery from a brain injury or not. Peace lies within. Strength lies within. Happiness lies within. May you find that which lies within you and may you know true freedom and contentment.

Chapter 17
Death Bed Thinking and the Language of Compromise

As wellbeing, interesting and hopefully inspirational for people into T'ai Chi and spiritual paths in life, this book is also intended as a kind of therapy for my fellow brain injury survivors; it is written, inevitably now, from the perspective of a survivor, a near-death-experience survivor no less. It's been an unpalatable truth that post-traumatic stress syndrome, surviving near death, facing my own mortality or however you put it, has put me at odds with the world that I once knew. It's as if I died, twice, and that I came back to a slightly, but profoundly different world to the one I left. Obviously, it's not the world that's changed significantly, it's me, or rather the way I process my experience of it.

Quite a bit is said about 'death bed thinking': what are the thoughts that you have when faced with possible, in my case probable death? I found that my focus was definitely towards the moments in life that I had felt most fulfilled. For most of my life I've been an actor so it's probably not surprising that my thoughts turned to the great moments of fulfilment on stage: the curtain call at the Garrick in the West End when I'd played the lead in 12 Angry Men was one such moment. I remember that last night standing backstage with Robert Vaughn (one of my boyhood heroes from The Magnificent Seven, to The Man from Uncle) "On you get Jason, you've earned it!" he said in that unique voice of his.

He was brilliant, how many times were we late onstage as he regaled us with stories of Steve McQueen and the golden bygone age of cinematic magnificence. Geoff Fahey said to me in rehearsal, "Spend time with Robert, listen to his stories, we don't know how long we have with him then he'll be gone". How prophetically true as we lost dear Robert shortly after our run of Angry Men closed. A true gentleman and a brilliant actor, on our last night, backstage, he turned to me and asked "Anything lined up for after?" "No Robert" I replied. "Me neither, but that's show business!" he quipped with that wry smile!

What's interesting about these death-bed thoughts, memories of time well-spent, of life being fulfilled is that my bank balance at that time was irrelevant, I have no idea if I was flush or not: it's of no consequence at all, all that mattered was the experience of that time, with those people, in that moment... And this causes a problem for those of us that are fortunate to come back from the brink of death; we learn the real value of life, which I'm afraid puts us at odds with most of humanity.

It seems to me that most people spend most of their time putting off fulfilment until this mundanity is achieved or that amount of money is secured, or the kids are all grown up or whatever. They worry about the good opinions of others and spend their lives in a kind of waking dream in which they serve a purpose of pleasing the conditions of life, or others place them under (they believe) until, faced with their last gasps they finally wake up to the fact that they have been in a kind of complicit fog their whole lives and that the things they really wanted to experience are now beyond them, it's too late: game over without even playing.

Most of us learn, or are taught from an early age a 'language of compromise' that sets us down the foggy road of people-pleasing. It happens when we're young. Often from well-meaning people such as parents or friends; we are taught to focus on what we can't do, on dangers, and difficulties. But, as has been said before, hunter-gatherers do not function in a state of fear. Take childhood tree-climbing as an example. We have our own self-preservation mapped into us. We also as a species have the need to explore and push the boundaries of exploration and danger. So, when a child climbs a tree, they don't need to hear "be careful darling!" they will be, naturally. But most well-meaning parents introduce an unnatural element of doubt and fear into a situation that was actually, and quite naturally under control.

This way of thinking then permeates out into the child's life and unless they are very brave, and unless they stand against that lonely tide, fear of life subtly grips them and they have these incessant doubt-filled whispers constantly prophesying to them "better not…just get this done and then…I can't do that" …and so on, and they **do**, ultimately, **nothing** of what they really want to do. Then they lie there, about to die, full of regrets that they didn't get to do the very thing that would have given them a sense of real fulfilment. And they die, full of confusion and resentment that the things they could have changed they didn't change. They stayed, stuck there until time ran its course, and ran out.

After their death the mundane things that they were taking care of with such martyrdom get done anyway. Or they don't. It's really of little consequence. It's just stuff, just things. Stuff and things get quickly forgotten and replaced because they have no real value. You might think that providing stuff and things will be appreciated by those you leave behind, but it's not the case because the material world has no intrinsic consequence to the sentient experience: only fulfilment of experiences in life does.

So how do we navigate the pressures of let's say family life with individual fulfilment? How do we know if we're pursuing the right goals in the first place? Perhaps we're just not good enough? I believe the answer to this lies within instinct similar to the child's survival and self-preservation instinct when climbing that tree: we are programmed, hard-wired to seek and to endure and to forebear and grow. The trick is to realise that whatever we focus upon will grow and multiply in our presence. It's just a question of right focus.

And don't misunderstand me there can be great fulfilment in simply providing for others, or finding beauty in the simplest of tasks, when done right and for the right reasons. It's really the quality of what we do that counts, that makes for fulfilment and joy. "Lo I have been selling water by the river, and have not sold a thing!" The end result doesn't matter, the joy and fulfilment in the process does. That's what is memorable. That is what makes for the death-bed thought. That time you felt great about being you.

The language of compromise disturbs your focus and concentration, makes you feel that what you're doing isn't enough, isn't good enough, isn't of enough value. So, when the doubts and fears pervade, you alter and change course steering instead through fissures chosen for you by the brief good intentions of others. The problem is that others only really ever start you off down a path and then leave you to it. And they then wonder why you via off course! Why you deviate and seem to revert to type…

Well, guess what, that's because they are wrong. Life's too short let me tell you from experience to live vicariously by another's idea of what is best for you, no matter how well intentioned their advice might be. Ultimately, only you can experience life through your receptors: you're the mind that then has to interpret meaning from the stimuli picked up by the receptors. So be sure that your instrumentation is finely tuned and ready to receive the myriad of messages that come for you, from deep within you, to bring you an abundance of joy and fulfilment.

You just simply need to shut out the other voices and listen to that tiny, thin, quietly unwavering voice of truth: your own personal reality that needs to be listened to with attentive clarity before it's too late. Before too much travelling has been done down those alien paths of another's choice. Don't allow it. Fight. Stand your ground.

Is it possible to fight and stand your ground peacefully and non-confrontationally though? Yes… It's a question of learning to listen to your inner-voice and intuition. Here, I find T'ai Chi and meditation to be of immense help: nothing grounds you in your own truth and power more than T'ai Chi, and meditating on the Qigong moves is the prefect focus for growth.

Meditating upon T'ai Chi is like watering the plants in a lovely garden, you don't actually see the plants and flowers grow and blossom, but they do. Critically here though is the quality and purity of the water with which you feed your garden. If you want abundance learn to keep the quality of your 'thought-water' pure.

Learn not to dilute your 'thought-water' with the ideas and thoughts of others. Keep yourself, your mind and spirit and body holy by feeding it what you know to be the good stuff! The stuff of life for you! Your truth is your own, so isn't it most sensible and simplest to be sure that you are actually in on the act? As I said, this doesn't have to be confrontational, often we just need to make a start down the path of freedom and everything else starts to fall into place. Trust your hunter-gatherer instincts and get doing some T'ai Chi and meditation sessions ASAP!

Chapter 18
T'ai Chi and the Art of Letting Go

Having a brain injury is certainly a tricky thing! The aftermath can be an overwhelming sense that this short life needs to be lived to the full with immediate effect, before it's too late! This can create a foreboding lack of self-worth that you're not doing enough things of great note, you're not leaving some kind of legacy of worthiness, or praiseworthy acts. That, in fact, you're a failure. Personally, in spite of my incredible physical recovery (I'm writing this chapter on June 15, 2022, so it's almost a year post-SAH…that's all) I still struggle with people. I seem to see and hear too acutely for this world and can become overwhelmed very easily by social situations, fluorescent lighting, intrusive background noise and the like. This makes normal life, and indeed the garnering of success as an actor or teacher terribly challenging.

It's as if I've become an incredible success story in terms of my physicality and the extremity of near-death survival; but I find thriving in the 'normal' world to be terribly difficult. I don't fit in with the ways of people, or with the ways of sight and sound produced by people; and I certainly don't feel like I fit in with society whilst 'carrying' around with me the extremity of my near-death experiences: the certain knowledge of a life beyond death that my 'fellow travellers' seem incapable of hearing of or engaging with comfortably. Perhaps that's only to be expected? I mean, my near-death experiences are like nothing I've read or heard of before and they don't exactly fit in with religious doctrines that I know of. But, moreover, as I've alluded to before in this book, I just don't think people generally want to be confronted with the stark realities of life and death: not really…And I get the sense that my very presence makes people uncomfortable. Maybe that's why I relate better to horses? I digress…

Perhaps when we identify what it is we 'want' from our lives and the possible methods we might employ to attain the desired outcome it is a temptation to become obsessed with an idealised image of a new life, new successes or new outcomes that we are so deserving of, now that we have come back from the brink of the abyss? Unfortunately, and somewhat ironically though, this way of thinking puts us at odds with the philosophy of T'ai Chi as it can form within us strong attachments to specific outcomes much akin to burning ambition or the attainment of material wealth and abundance.

I say it's ironic because without doubt, near-death-experiences get you thinking about the 'important' stuff in your life, but we must be very careful not to engage with a style of thinking which inculcates judgements of success and failure, in turn creating stress and anxiety that you've yet to achieve this or that, and that life is short and that time is running out. This way of thinking is not reserved, of course, just for survivors of NDEs. And it's not that goals or ambitions are wrong per se: however, attachments to outcomes which are actually often unrealistic expectations can become extremely dangerous psychologically for us all.

Whether you've had a brain injury or not, stress and anxiety are unhelpful states of being. How do we do it then? How can we make each moment count, how can we live our best lives and be our most authentic selves without getting stressed that 'life' or the 'rest of the world' isn't going along with our new-found philosophy? Didn't I nearly die? Shouldn't everything and everyone make things easy for me now? Don't I deserve all of the successes and abundance that life can offer? The answer is yes and no! In terms of T'ai Chi, no one moment is more or less valuable or beautiful than any other moment. They're just moments that pass with the breath and the movements of Qigong.

For moments to pass in peace and harmony they must not have barbs upon them of expectation and desire. This is true for Qigong and meditation alike. Freedom requires a healthy lack of care about outcomes, a healthy disregard for the 'valuable' and 'precious'. Things are just things. Stuff is just stuff. Moments are just moments. Each singular moment having equal opportunity for love and caring. Each moment having as much potential as the next to be exquisitely perfect; as long as we remain unattached to its exquisite beauty and perfection. This is the great irony: to live a life of true freedom and integrity we have to let go of attachments to outcomes: simple, and yet ridiculously difficult!

Imagine a stream flowing through a mountain pass. The stream represents both T'ai Chi Qigong and meditation practice and the flow of life itself. Imagine the clear water burbling over the stones, mud, silt, and organisms on the bed of the stream. To the water, what it travels over is of no importance as it weaves down the mountain. It's doing what a stream does. Flowing downwards ever downwards towards the larger river

162

and eventually out to the sea. If a discarded old bike frame has been thrown into the stream-bed, the water still flows just the same as ever, it makes no difference to the water.

And if, instead of the bike frame there was a precious diamond or gold bar in the bed of the stream, the water would still flow, just as before: irrespective of what lies beneath the surface of the water, the water still flows no matter what. In a way this is the ultimate aim of T'ai Chi and meditation and the ultimate aim for life: to become like the water of a mountain stream, flowing over everything with equality and integrity.

Everything that life throws into our path, each object or obstruction, each dilemma or lack of opportunity, each moment of greatness or moment of nothingness should be treated with equal regard or disregard. It's all one. Nothing is of any greater value than anything else. Everything is beautiful. Each moment is magical. Life is either a miraculous incredible gift in every waking and sleeping second or it is not...to consistently achieve this way of thinking we have to let go. We have to let go of attachments to people, things, and outcomes. We have to let go…

If you've come close to death, like me, then you'll be acquainted with letting go. There was a point with me when I had to come to terms with the very real possibility that I was going to lose my life and that all of my wants and desires would come to nothing. In a way it was a strangely liberating experience. The ultimate letting go. I came to the realisation that all of the 'stuff' that was going on with me would get taken care of without me. The story of my life would continue to be told by those mourning my death. The immediacy of each moment in intensive care is actually something to be treasured. I mean imagine that you feel right now, genuinely, that these might be your last minutes, hours, or days to live. Doesn't that make each breath strangely sweeter? Each sunrise more awe-inspiring?

I found myself not in a fight or flight situation, but a fight or fight-a-bit-harder one. When you're truly cornered thinking becomes crystal-clear and choices, as stark as it sounds, are made so much easier when the stakes are at their very highest. So, I guess I kind of got used to death, I got used to the idea of having to fight and fight just to get to the next moment, the next hour, the next day. And in a way, as difficult as it's been to recover physically, it's where I'm at now, mentally that I find so very hard to deal with. If life just consisted of the extremity, the precipice, the edge of the abyss, I think I'd see things more clearly and excel in a primitive kind of way. Is it because I've tasted death, is that what makes the minutia complexities of life so hard to handle? I confess for much of the time I feel like an alien species in a foreign land.

These are the things I can do, none of which incidentally helps me get back into society: T'ai Chi Qigong, ride horses, spend time with horses! Maybe that's ok?

And I guess that's why I've written this book, to try to reach out to others who might have gone through similar things or who identify with some of the philosophies or sentiments here? I truly hope that you find something in these pages to be helpful and inspiring.

Part 2

Preface

Every culture, religion, creed and tradition has its stories of beasts and monsters; of fear and overcoming; of belief in the face of the unknown terror. Many of these traditions are actually a form of representation of the human condition and are symbolic in their context of the trials and tribulations of existence and the afterlife. Gargoyles, monsters, angels, devils, gnomes, warlocks, wicked witches and sorcerers; journeys taken by heroes and heroines to save decaying kingdoms that are riven with betrayal and conceit are representative of an individual's journey, navigating the turbulent waters of life and death.

I first wrote this short story in the 90s following the tragic death of a friend who actually did fall from a speeding Inter City train. To this day the circumstances of her death remain a mystery and thinking about it now, I guess I wrote the story not just as a reaction to her tragic life being cut short so terribly, so pointlessly and so violently; but also, as a means to exorcise my own feelings of fear and anger that all life, and all that we value and love, will one day be taken away. No one has ever read it before but I thought to include it here because re-reading it again since my brain injury—so much of it is a pretty colourful analogous look at the nature of death within society as a whole and our spiritual, ethical and religious reaction to it.

You can tell that it's written in the early 90s with all of the references to smoking in pubs!

The characters themselves are best thought of as symbolic representations of the human psyche: namely mine. The Man and the darkness that pervades throughout the story is emblematic of the fear that death and the unknown holds over us sentient beings; much of the winter weather in the story represents the difficulties and struggles we face when considering our own mortality in respect of life's journey and just how 'wintery' our thinking is most of the time.

The references to organised religion reflect my thoughts then and now of how little morality or the spiritual teachings of the church have helped me in my struggles with the questions raised by my own existence and future demise. The afterlife sections, whilst being indicative of most peoples' imaginings are not accurate in terms of my actual recent near-death experiences. I've elected, however, to keep it as is so as to not disrupt the flow of the story or the underlying authorial intent from all of those years ago.

Sometimes thinking again can be a problem for us brain injury survivors. Contemplating what we've been through and how close we came to death can be overwhelming and terrifying. But we need to find a way to think about things again: a way to think about life and death in abstracted concepts again. Like fairy stories and other traditions enable, this story encapsulates the wonder and terror of life and death in iconographic images that mimic life's journey without making it so stark and real.

This short story is simply a metaphor for life's questions and potential answers; life's journey. It is intended in the context of this book as a kind of brain-gym, a means by which you can practice seeing meaning in the metaphorical and abstract again without feeling worried or uptight about the reality of how close brain injury took you to the abyss, to death.

I hope you enjoy the story, although it is intended as a springboard for thought and ideas more than a completed story in the traditional sense: it lacks beginning, middle and end—the intention being that you see the meaning and fill in the blanks for yourself.

The Soulscape

A Graphic, Symbolic Short Story

Chapter 1

1.

My name is Christine.

I remember, as a little girl, sitting with my parents on a train. I was two. No, perhaps **remember** is the wrong word, perhaps "see" would be more accurate— it's hard for me to describe something to you that's outside all human experiences, by definition it's indescribable.

Anyway, there I am with my parents looking out of the window shouting; "train, train — one, two..." And as the second train passes, I'm laughing and jumping.

"What colour is that train, Christine, sweetheart ?" My father asks.

I say, "Blue."

Those are happy sights. I ask if I may see them again and again—occasionally they let me but mostly they make me see this:

I'm older, 19 years older and I'm sitting on a train looking out of the window. Under my breath I utter the words "one...two...blue." I laugh out loud and the man next to me shuffles uncomfortably. "Trains make me giggle," I say.

"Oh," the man says, looking embarrassed. Apart from the man and me the train is deserted.

I take a magazine from my carrier bag and my blue, plastic, rail-card wallet falls out. I put it in the back pocket of my jeans.

I randomly flick through the pages of the magazine until I come to two pages bizarrely stuck together at the top like Siamese twins. "A clever marketing ploy?" I ask myself. I gently ease the pages apart and see the picture of a beautiful woman on a tropical, white-sanded, parched-looking beach. She has long blonde hair, dark brown skin and is wearing a white swimsuit. She has a dark-skinned, blonde-haired (am I meant to believe she's hers?) child with her.

None of this is particularly out of keeping with this manner of literature — the striking thing is that the pair of them look so astonishingly at peace. Not just as the contented mother and daughter pair that they are meant to be portraying, but more so individually, independently they look serene. They almost appear to be floating in the hot, deep-blue sky.

Oh God it looks truly beautiful. I want children. I want two, no four and I want a dog and a land-rover and a husband…and I want the loo.

I fall on the man half on purpose as I get up, "Sorry," I say.

"Quite all right," the man says looking more than embarrassed.

I could sometimes do that to men.

Immediately as I come out of the loo we go into a tunnel and the train goes dark. It seems to speed up, clattering from side to side — a strange sensation in the blinding black.

Losing my balance, I reach out in panic and grab someone's arm to steady myself.

"Sorry," I say .

The next thing I feel is a hand on my throat and a searing cold wind ripping through the carriage.

"What? What?"

The hand covers my mouth, my feet leave the ground and I start to fly in the cold.

I see the brown girl, the serene sky, the blue train.

I see my father, ("one") and I hear me laugh when I'm two.

Now there's fear, acute white fear.

"I'm falling."

"I'm going to die."

"Oh no, oh please!"

"Mummy, Daddy."

"Help!"

"HELP!"

"One…two…blue…"

Silence.

Silence.

Flames of white with an intensity beyond mere light or colour rocket me forwards. I'm racing, careering into what must be oblivion. Unbearably loud bells are peeling, screeching my approach.

Faster and faster.

Scream. Scream.

I stop.

The light becomes broader and fuller with no end. And I'm vast, as huge as the universe. I hear strange music and men singing. I feel warmer now.

I look down and I see me on the ground. And then I'm there, next to me. My legs are curled around my back and my face is cut.

I feel cold.

There's my plastic wallet on the ground.

Somehow, I'm back on the train and there's the man going to his seat.

"Did you do this?"

"Did you kill me?"

"Oh, Daddy help me."

I'm back in the endless white and the voices start calling me, singing to me.

"NO. NO!"

I try to scream.

The voices stop.

There's a door.

I go through it.

2.

Look at this pure colour for example. It's yellow, isn't it? Well, yes, we can agree that you've learned to recognise those signals as yellow, but if you could get inside someone's head might they not really be seeing red and merely calling it yellow, at least the way that you see yellow through your eyes?

Now imagine that all of the thoughts and perceptions of everyone who ever lived become living entities after their deaths. And imagine that the lust for knowledge is the driving life-force of all of these entities and that gradually after their physical deaths, each entity is able to "see" more and more through the "eyes" of each other entity that ever existed. And imagine that as each entity gets closer and closer to ultimate truth, it is dividing itself again and again. And as the power of truth becomes stronger the "self" becomes weaker and more distant.

Feelings do not exist here, nor do memories, nor do hopes. There is no past or future here, there is only this place and the place itself is only defined by the particles who haven't divided themselves enough to know that a "space", or "place" is not necessary, nor is it truth.

I'm just starting.

If you were here, which is of course ridiculous, you'd probably see this place as black. You'd be cold I think, and you would be profoundly, desperately, horribly lonely.

I know all of this because I'm just starting. They told me this would be how I would feel for as long as my feelings continued to exist. As I divide, my feelings and memories and dreams are gradually subsiding. I sometimes have flashes of panic; I want to scream "Oh God" but I realise that's ridiculous too…

I seem to have been here forever, evaporating or dividing or whatever they call it …

They're all over me, around me, in me, I'm like a tiny pebble in a sand-storm and they're trapping me here the bastards. Get out of me you little shits …

I'm finding it harder to think, to think about me, who I am. I know I feel a little bit sad; I'm forgetting why. Occasionally I see glimpses.

Sunlight streams in through the broken window of the little wooden shed. Particles of dust dance like sparklers within the golden columns. It smells of creosote. I like it. My cheek flattens itself on the dusty floor. Might there be spiders? Don't move. Don't even breathe. Stay silent. Hide.

Suddenly, the door swings open and an 8-year-old cowboy is framed in the yellow haze. He is dressed in white from Stetson to spurs, except for a bright red bandanna tied neatly around his neck. He smiles.

"That's not fair, that's just not bloody fair!" I protest in a rage.

The little boy laughs hysterically, takes his gun from his holster, says, "I win" and shoots …

3.

That's the sun… Yes, it is. I can feel it warming my back. But surely, I've forgotten, or evaporated too much to feel things, or to care?

There's sand in my hands and under my fingernails, itching me. I turn over and open my eyes and I'm blinded by a hot sun.

"I don't understand"

"It's O.K."— a man's voice .

I sneeze.

As my pupils gradually adjust themselves to the light, I can see a calm red sea only yards from me. A little wave laboriously gathers momentum, speeds towards me, pauses for a moment and then changes its mind.

"It's really O.K" sitting next to me, looking out at the blank, rouged horizon is a man in his early thirties. He has dark skin (the kind you get from lying on a beach all day) black curly hair, shorts, brown leather flip-flops and a white shell necklace. He is the most beautiful man I've ever seen. He looks at me, he has kind and strangely calming deep brown, almost black/brown eyes and a slight stubble protruding from his weather-beaten, tanned face.

He smiles.

Silence.

He turns, crouches on his heels, selects a flat pebble and skims it at the sea as if to shock the slowly approaching waves into a snap decision — they retreat, to prepare for another futile onslaught.

I look around me. Apart from the beautiful man and myself, the beach is deserted. There isn't a clump of grass, or a bird, or anything other than the white sand, brown pebbles and us. It's all so very uninterrupted. Even the sea seems "turned down", making its sojourns to the shore in a reverential hush.

I'm wearing my old black bikini, the one I wore in Greece that time and the same beaded necklace and the same silver bracelet… "Where are we?"

The man is silent.

"Look, please, I'm frightened, I don't understand. Please just tell me where I am."

"Come with me."

The beautiful man takes me by the hand and slowly we meander along the shore. The parching sun bakes my back and the almost smouldering sand scorches the soles of my feet. To cool down we paddle through the shallows, the inviting sea gently kissing our ankles as we stroll, hand-in-hand along the white, faultless beach.

"Am I in Heaven?"

"What do you think?"

"I think I miss my parents and my friends."

"I know"… he stares at me with an intensity that pierces through my eyes, through my head, down the inside of my body, into what I can only describe as "me". I feel invaded again, like I did in the dividing room.

He looks away.

"We're nearly there," he says with a gentle smile.

We walk on, he occasionally bending down to throw another pebble into the mumbling sea. The sullen sun remains suspended, motionless, as if pinned on to the basking sky.

Suddenly the flat, endless, desert-like beach, transforms itself into huddles of giant circular rocks jutting out through the sea into the endless firmament beyond. We hop from one rock to the other, going further and further out to sea, until we come to a shallow sand bank where fathoms of sea-water condenses into a couple of inches. We jump down. We're in the middle of the sea. Before us are three huge caves. The sea quietly slashes their walls with its lap, lap, as the sun is banished into shadow by the caves 'dank interiors, dripping their chilling welcome. He sits on a rock looking into the caves, I sit down with him and this is what he tells me:

"These two caves are here to help you. The first one will take you back to what you call the dividing room where you will gain ultimate knowledge and attain your true eternal state which, at present, you are denying yourself. Soon your thirst for truth will bring you back to us, but we appreciate that you must first understand and then embrace what has happened to you.

"Entry into the second cave will allow you to "see" again your time on Earth and in particular your last hours alive. You will re-experience again and again your life, and your death. It will all appear to you as reality, as if it were happening to you right now. You will simply re-live passages of your life and your death until you are ready to let go. Whilst "re-living" you will be unaware that you are dead. Only when you return here will you become aware of and able to understand more about the change you have undergone.

"Until you complete this change by entering the "dividing room" you will remain here "in between". If you were to go into the second cave now it would be the tenth time that you have revisited the shadows of the past, of your life. You are gradually learning to finish what has already ended. Sometimes, like this time you will learn and attain nothing, you will only experience the change brought about by your death. Sometimes it will all be much clearer to you.

"When you have "seen" enough you will enter the first cave and join us.

"The third cave you must not enter.

"Think of this as a detour on your journey, a place to contemplate what you have still to learn.

"When you know enough, you will join us."

Chapter 2

"This is a new one," Martin Daniels thought to himself as he attempted to negotiate the creaking wheelchair, with its equally "creaking" occupant into the Auxiliary Lift of St. Margaret's Hospital.

"This is definitely a new one."

In fact, it was from some thirty or forty feet away that he'd first spotted the new recruit. Over the years he'd learned to recognise each chair with its individual markings and idiosyncrasies; to know whether it was a right-wheeler or a left-wheeler...As far as hospital porters go Martin was silent when compared to the others' "taxi driver-like" chat. He preferred it that way. To be invisible you have to be silent.

In the lift, between the ground floor and the third floor, was the only time he ever really spoke to anyone. He knew that any lack of response from the man or woman he was pushing was probably only due to the fact that they were desperately saving each breath, unsure as to whether it would be their last. It was not because they didn't understand. On the contrary, he knew they were the only ones who ever could understand. To be near to the very elderly or mentally ill patients gave him a sense of comfort. They all understood.

As he came out of the lift he turned left, as usual, to go to the hospice. En route he slowed, as usual, to peer into ward three — the maternity ward. To him, this place was one of particular comfort and of particular pain. During the times when the men came back (often with their little gifts) and both parents were reunited with their new-borns, Martin would watch with great joy, with great pride. Until, inevitably, a protective father would notice him and instruct a nurse to "Get rid of that weirdo."

The nurses, who had grown used to Martin, would explain to the irate fathers that he was harmless but usually Martin would be asked by a kindly patronising voice, to leave. When, however, he watched the parents of a still-born baby or a baby rapidly approaching death in an incubator, his secure position of "invisible man" would be restored to him and his tears would be undetected by parents who were diluting the world with their own.

As usual he stopped the wheelchair outside the large hall window of the maternity ward. Today's "passenger" had been asleep for two weeks, a couple of minutes pause on his journey would be of little consequence to him.

Martin tried to look through the window as if he wasn't. His view, though, was blocked by sunlight streaming in through the outer ward window creating a type of yellow mirror of the hall window, enabling him to see only a jaundiced reflection of himself.

At first, he didn't recognise the face staring back at him. He hadn't really "looked" at himself in ten years. But today he was shocked into looking. He was trapped there. Like the gnarled trunk of a petrified tree, he was frozen to the spot.

The helpless expression on his once hopeful face told him the sickening truth, that the dolorous wound dealt him all those years ago had finally severed the last sinews of his heart and it was bleeding heavily. It was draining every drop of life from him. His bent, skeletal, defeated frame bore sad witness to the pathetic fact that he was still (albeit only just) alive.

"What a terrible state to be in at thirty-five," he concluded, adding "I'm an old man". His once blue-black hair was fading to ash. The features of his face jutted-out and sunk-in like the smashed hull of an ancient ship and his eyes as grey as clouds, seemed constantly to be preparing for a downpour of tears. He wore the scars that had savagely lacerated this quiet man on his sleeve for all to see. Not because he wanted the world to acknowledge or to somehow share his troubles, but simply because his pain was too great to contain. Pain poured out and overflowed from him with an unstoppable ferocity, burning his already charred insides with eruptions of terrible, terminal, suffering.

He saw a terrified expression on the face of the man in the wheelchair who had woken and was looking up at him. This old man was the real reflection of Martin Daniels. They were both waiting for death.

Martin gently placed his hand on the old man's shoulder. They understood. Time would not cure, nor would it heal, it would simply snuff out their existence leaving only the fading embers of memories in those who knew them. As he gazed into the ancient eyes, Martin thought, "Perhaps no-one will remember me? Yes, by now it wouldn't surprise me if no-one noticed I'd gone. I'll disappear like a tiny pebble falling into a vast ocean."

The old man escaped into sleep once more and Martin resumed their journey, deliberately ignoring the jaundiced face of the figure in the window "ghosting" him …

But the yellow man leapt out of the window onto his back. He began to crush Martin's skull with his blank hands, harder and harder. With each tentative, excruciating step, he drove Martin backwards, year by year, back to before the time of pain. Back to life.

"Why do I have to go through it again? Why? I don't want to. If I have to watch myself die each time, why can't you just let me die? Why do you have to hurt me again and again…?"

Ten years ago, things were different. For a brief time, a gust of happiness blew into the life of the quiet, frightened young man.

Her name was Christine.

Chapter 3

University as a 25-year-old felt like defeat to Martin before he'd started—especially a scared 25-year-old. It appeared to him as if the entire population of "cool" under 21-year-olds had enrolled at the University. He stood outside the front gates. Like standing in the centre of a vast merry-go-round where thousands of riders bustle up and down and round and round, or like a terrified rabbit facing the headlights of rapidly approaching traffic, it was only a matter of time before all of this would send him flying. There he was beached, stranded at the entrance of the University like so much unwanted driftwood conspicuously washed up on this alien shore.

"Fortune favours the brave!"

"Um?"

"Fortune favours the brave — it's a famous saying, not that I can remember who said it, except my Dad says it all the time, not that he's famous, or fortunate …, oh well ! My name's Christine. What course are you on?"

Freshers charged passed them occasionally knocking one or other of them off balance. The constant nervous noise of masses of people meeting each other for the first time (and all trying too hard) seemed to subside into distant barks and yelps. From the one glimpse his fear had allowed him of her he'd established that she was stunningly beautiful and therefore had concluded that he would securely pack any notions of "girlfriend" away with the rest of the capacity filled "baggage" he hauled around with him.

"Geography."

"You've come here to study geography and you seem unable to find your way to the right course! That's pretty funny don't you think?"

"Um!"

"I'm doing English along with the rest of the known world. God, I hate crowds. Don't you?"

"Yes."—How refreshing perhaps his claustrophobic—agoraphobia would be a conversation starter this time instead of its usual wet-blanket-smother-and-extinguish-effect— "I do get a bit claustro—"

"Tell me. If you're on a really crowded train that has arrived at its 'destination, do you (A) get up quickly and rush off battling through the queue, or (B) sit where you are and let everyone else get off first?"

"Um, B"

"Me too, I used to try to be an A, but I gave it up and now I'm most definitely a B." She laughed the kind of laugh you remember for the rest of your life.

She wore no make-up. She smiled a lot. She had brown hair and blue eyes. She wore hiking boots, jeans, a white t-shirt and a brown leather jacket. Her extreme beauty made it impossible to take her all in in one glance and (along with the rest of them) Martin was staring at her.

He became self-conscious, suddenly aware that he (the walking cliché with corduroy jacket and patched jeans to-boot) had immediately fallen stupidly in love with a girl who in two weeks' time would smile "hello" whilst holding hands with Steve, or Danny, or Gary, or anybody else but him. He looked away, desperately wanting the ground to swallow him and his "man from Oxfam" outfit up.

"What did you say your name was?"

"Um Martin Daniels"—Damn, why do I have to say "um" before everything? It makes me sound like I don't know anything for certain. Am I unsure of my own name? —These thoughts progressed into panic as an impossible silence ensued …

He courageously tried to think of something interesting to say.

"Um," was the predictable result.

"What's the time?"

"Um nine thirty-one."

"Oh shit, we're late. Listen, I imagine you're in the same boat as me—first day, don't know anyone all of that, so do you fancy meeting up at lunchtime? Back here? That is of course if our famous geography student can find his way back!" That laugh again.

She ran off and was absorbed into the hordes, vanishing as if she were an illusion. Martin assumed that he would never see her again and like Helen of Troy, he filed her memory under "L" for "legend".

What time was "lunch time"? To be on the safe side he decided to set the broadest perimeters so that if (by some quirk of fate) she did turn up, he would definitely not miss her due to confusion over what was the accepted hour for luncheon. He concluded that waiting from eleven until three would be reasonable.

He felt a bit like a naughty schoolboy bunking off a lesson to have a cigarette behind the bike sheds. Not that he'd ever smoked or played truant before (before now) but nevertheless he imagined that this is what it would feel like.

What an odd day! To arrive at a university and to immediately manage to talk to a beautiful girl (in his case a feat worthy of the Victoria Cross!) yet to have not yet managed to actually enter the University buildings.

He was sure people must have thought he was the gardener, standing in the same spot all morning trying to remember where he'd left his rake.

"How long have you been waiting here?" —One o'clock! One o'clock is lunch time!

"Um , oh , um ,…five minutes …"

"You look quite shocked , has anything happened?"

"Yes…,I mean no, no, everything's fine."

"There's a pub around the corner, do you fancy a drink and a sandwich there?"

"Yes, yes. That would be very nice."

Perhaps "fortune" could turn her back on the 'brave' and favour the 'extremely hopeful' for a change?

Chapter 4

"I'm going to go back now. Into the first cave, all right?"

"I don't know. I, I'm scared, I don't want to be alone."

"You're not alone. I promise you."

"Will I see you again?"

"Yes."

The beautiful man turned from Christine and looked into the shadows of the cave. He walked away from her. The water became deeper the further into the giant tunnel he went.

At the point when he was wading with the water at chest height the cave became illuminated by dancing flashes of colours—bright and radiant shades of reds, pinks, blues, greens and tinged whites whose vibrant energies seemed not to be coming from any particular source but all seemed independently 'alive'.

Soon he was surrounded by millions upon millions of these shimmering entities. Waves of sound echoed around the cave. Deep, low a-tonal sound the production of which emanated from this eternal wall of colours whose brilliance and magnitude now blanked the huge cave from view, engulfing every molecule of space in the entire universe perhaps, as they multiplied over and over again. Higher pitched sounds modulated around the lower tones, increasing its strange intensity, throbbing with life.

The enchanting music was unremittingly gentle and it filled Christine with a sense of profound peace. She desired to join them. Never before had she experienced desire like it. She wanted to leap into the warm depths and be there with them. She approached the wall of light. She slowly, tentatively put her hand into the vast cacophony of colour and sound. It was warm in there and it was beautiful and it was peaceful. Then the sonorous melodies began to fade and, in their place, came voices, soft, barely audible voices whispering her name.

"Christine, come now. Come now. Come into the Dividing Room and be with us."

Christine put her other hand into the "wall". The need to be with them, to walk into and to become one with this kaleidoscope of swirling "peacefulness" was immense and apparently unquenchable. She knew that going through the Dividing Room meant saying goodbye to her life and to herself, to her feelings and to her body (or whatever it was she now inhabited) forever.

She was ready. She would join them now.

Then she heard an alien sound — under these circumstances it was a strangely ordinary alien sound:

"Clackaty-clack, clackaty-clack" followed by laughter. The laughter of a little girl.

"Look Daddy , look….There's a blue train … one…two…"

Christine pulled her hands from the wall and sank to her knees.

The colours, the music and her peace evaporated.

She was alone.

She cried for the loss of her life.

She cried for the restless uncertainties she was tormented with in her death.

She ran out of the first cave and into the second. Falling as the water got deeper, she charged into its dark interior. Eventually her feet no longer touched the bottom and she was dragged along by a powerful current.

After what felt like miles the water became shallower until it was a mere trickle running through a large, damp, cold 'room' in the bowels of the cave. Directly in front of her was a bluish shimmering 'colour'.

"Um, I'd like to go home please. I'd just like to see it again," she wept.

The 'colour' grew and grew revealing a hole, like a tear in a sheet, in its centre. As the tear became larger warm air wafted through it from the other side. Christine could hear footsteps and a man's voice above a hubbub of background voices and music coming from the world beyond the tear.

"Do you really want to go back that far again Christine?" It was the beautiful man again; he was standing behind her.

"Listen, it's all right for you, you've accepted all of this, I can't. I want to know why. Why did I have to die like that? Who did this to me? Was it that guy on the train or was there someone else? Why?"

"I don't know."

"Well I swear, as futile as it is to return to my life each time knowing that I have to go through death, each time...I swear that I will not rest until I find out why this happened to me. Why?"

He said nothing in the most tender way that it is possible to say nothing.

Christine turned her back on the beautiful man and without looking back, she climbed through the tear.

"A pint of bitter and a half of lager, please." Christine peered across the crowded pub and waved a type of "I've finally been served" wave to Martin. He smiled a type of "Oh well, not to worry" smile and then looked away in order to continue his giant apology to the world for his existence. Christine liked him.

She arrived back with their drinks and sat next to the shy, charming young man. She stared at him and then she smiled.

Chapter 5

Martin felt very uncomfortable sitting alone whilst Christine bought him his pint of bitter in the claustrophobic, smoke-filled pub. His sense of discomfiture was augmented by what he looked like. He was filled with dread at the thought of being the only "fashion leper" in a pub that seemed to be holding a convention for "hip" people. He was sure that every conversation in the over-crowded bar was about him. He heard a female voice rise above the white noise with a "have you seen?" followed by an astonished laugh. Yes, it was all definitely about him!

How could a girl like Christine possibly want to spend more time than was absolutely necessary with him?

Christine waved to Martin from the bar and mouthed something to him. He couldn't quite understand but he smiled and waved back and then, not knowing what to do next, he looked away catching the eye of the girl on the adjacent table as he did, who looked from him to Christine and then back to her "cool" boyfriend with a nod and a knowing laugh.

Christine arrived back with their drinks and sat next to him.

She stared at him for a-heart-stopping-while and then she smiled.

"You are the most beautiful girl in the world," Martin thought to himself, daring to look at her once more, then adding with deep regret, "and I know that you will never love me".

He took as many gulps of beer as is possible to take whilst attempting to disguise them as a single first mouthful.

"So what are you like, eh? Who is Martin Daniels?" She put on a "cod" American "tacky gameshow host" type of accent.

He concluded that perhaps she was mocking him.

"Now don't tell me you're normal, or ordinary, or average" (she continued, fortifying the caricature) "because, hell, I just don't believe that of anybody, Goddammit!"

He wanted to join in the game but his intent faded, as did his appalling American accent after the first few words:

"Well, I think, I think I'm a bit shy…and I think I'm also, probably, a bit scared of all of this."

"All of what?" The gameshow host was growing into a psycho-analyst.

"Um…well , everyone else seems to be confident and sure of themselves and I, well I feel so incredibly nervous and ridiculous all the time and I, I, I, well, I just keep on asking myself "What am I doing here?"

"And what are you doing here?" She adopted her own voice and a serious, searching tone that made her questioning sound sincere, albeit deliberately ambiguous.

"Geography."

She laughed that abandoned, delicious laugh and shook her head, creating petite ripples in the wash of raven hair which shone despite the haloes of grey pub smoke that billowed around it.

"Bloody geography!"

He smiled.

Everyone else seemed to fade into the nicotine smog as the world outside of them diminished to mute. She was the only thing that existed. The only thing that he would ever want to exist.

There was a comfortable silence.

"What's your favourite book? And don't tell me the "World Atlas"!"

"Sorry?"

"It's all right, just another lame geography joke. Well?"

Martin desperately tried to think of the title of a book, any book, whether he'd read it or not. He couldn't.

"Well , what's your favourite book?" he retorted as casually as he could, implying that in the meantime he would sift through the mountainous bibliography of book titles that he knew, she knew, he didn't know!

"Oh, you'll think it's pretty boring, I don't mean a boring book, just a boring, common choice."

"I'm sure I won't."

"Well, it's "Wuthering Heights", I know, the usual choice of all of us love-sick "girlies" but there you are, my favourite book, of all time, is "Wuthering Heights.""

"Why?"

"Why? Why? Well, it's not because, as a lot of people mistakenly think, it's a soppy romance novel, I think it's more of a Gothic ghost story, but anyway, it's more to do with its, its hugeness. Do you know what I mean? I mean, the emotions of Cathy and Heathcliff are as extreme and as massive as the wild landscape they inhabit. Everything they do or say is of Titanic importance and they are prepared to follow everything that they decide to do through to the bitter end, regardless of the eventual consequences."

She took a quick passionate swig of lager. An amber bead trickled down the side of her chin, she wiped it away with the back of her hand.

"And the love that Heathcliff has for Cathy is so enormous that, basically, he kills her (not directly but he does) because she's married Edgar and she won't be, can't be with Heathcliff, even though she knows he is part of her soul. Heathcliff goes against her wishes and tries to get her back even though she's married, and he ends up fighting her husband. By turning against her and her wishes he destroys the part of her soul that is Heathcliff and by doing so he destroys her."

A mist of sweat like morning dew appeared on her forehead. She was either unaware of it or ignored it, either way Martin liked that.

"When she dies though, he curses her saying that she will never rest in death as long as he is alive and that he wants her to be with him as a ghost for the rest of his natural life, until they can finally be together in death. And for the rest of his life, he becomes like a monster, savagely intent on being revenged upon Edgar and all of his relatives, blaming them for changing her, taming her and eventually killing her.

"When Heathcliff is revenged upon them all and holds everyone at his mercy, he still can find no peace and is haunted by images of Cathy wherever he goes. He must have loved her more than anyone has ever loved before. You know, when he first learns of her death he becomes like a possessed animal, screaming: "I cannot live without my life. I cannot live without my soul.""

"Well anyway, it's a lot more complicated than that, obviously and I didn't describe it all that well because I get too excited whenever I get into "Wuthering Heights" but that's kind of the gist of why I love it so much."

Silence.

"How did Heathcliff kill her?"

"He broke her heart."

"I'd like to read it one day."

"I'll lend it to you."

Silence.

Silence.

Martin looked at his watch. It was three-thirty.

"Um , would you like another drink?"

"Yes , that would be lovely, thank you."

Martin struggled to his feet and squeezed through the masses.

He wanted her. He wanted her to be his and at this juncture how much she wanted him was not a factor that would sway him from his sacred intent.

For the first time in his life, he felt strong. He had a purpose, a quest, and he would never waver from "her" path. He would love her to the exclusion of all others and eventually, when presented day and night with his undying, faithful, all-consuming love, she would learn to love him too.

"Same again is it love?" the haughty blond barmaid snapped him back into reality.

"Oh, yes, I think so, hold on, I'll just check." Inwardly thanking the barmaid for giving him another chance to smile at Christine and to see her smile back at him, he turned, but

Christine had gone. Perhaps she had just been an illusion, a cruel mirage sent by an angry god to torture him.

Or perhaps she had just gone to the toilet! Yes, that must be it.

"Well love?" The barmaid quizzically glowered at him with an expression of: "You're not the only one in here you know!"

"Um , yes , same again please."

He returned to their table with their drinks and sat in her empty chair. He could smell the remnants of "her". Not her perfume, she didn't wear, it was "essence of her" that flavoured the air that she had previously occupied.

He fixed his eyes on the door to the lady's toilet. Two "designer girls" went in and a few minutes later came out.

He looked at his watch. It must have been fifteen minutes since he'd been at the bar. "Where on Earth could she be?"

"She's gone darling." It was the girl from the adjacent table, looking at him with a pitiful expression of, "You didn't really think she could ever want you, did you?"

"Where?"

"How the hell should I know. She just got up and charged out, nearly sent my bleedin 'drink flying." She turned back to her boyfriend with that knowing giggle. The same knowing giggle that he could hear all around him, from everyone. They had all been listening in and now they were all laughing at him.

He struggled out of the pub as quickly as he could.

Outside the light had faded prematurely to night. It was bitterly cold and it had been snowing heavily for some time. The cars drove by in slow motion so as not to skid on the drifted road. He began his weary trudge home to his newly rented

197

small, cold, damp bedsit, his feet sinking deeper into the crisp, freezing snow with every anguished step.

Where could she be?

Perhaps she's in some kind of trouble? If only he had her phone number, he could call her and check that she was all right. Perhaps she'd just got bored with his company and left when she had the chance. Back to her boyfriend no doubt. Back to her "cool" boyfriend when she sensed his undying love for her. She had read his mind while he was at the bar and scarpered. Back to her boyfriend.

The snowfall became a blizzard blanking-out the orange glow from the street-lights, creating a wilderness of white.

He was alone creeping through the barren wastes with only the top half of parked cars giving him any reference to the path beneath.

By the time he reached the front door of the Victorian house (that had been converted into as many bedsits as you could cram under its leaking hundred-year-old roof) his feet felt like clubs within his snow-filled shoes and his fingers barely possessed the requisite dexterity to put the key into the lock. The blood in his body felt congealed solid by the beating snow and cutting arctic wind.

He tortuously climbed the stairs barely able to lift his ravaged limbs, his face now burning from exposure to the punishing, frosted gale.

He sat on the end of the too-soft ancient bed in the too-small freezing bedsit with its peeling walls, single chest of drawers, wooden chair and one ring oven. He lay down on his back, saturating the previously dank bedclothes and plummeted into deep, desperate sleep.

Some dreams are good. Others are nightmares. Occasionally dreams can be more real than reality. They can seem to be a distilled, pure, white, inevitable version of things—and these dreams can be truly terrifying with their apparent harsh, cutting, unclouded, focused statements of ultimate truths. They are so very, very, very convincing. And they can, under the right convincing conditions, become your waking belief. Your reality: your life.

As some dreams do, it began with a replication of the events immediately preceding sleep: he fell asleep in his clothes, defrosting on the too-soft bed in the dingy bedsit, alone and afraid. A single thud on his door woke him.

Shivering, not wandering who it could be but weather he really did hear someone knock at his door at whatever time it was in the freezing black, he felt his way from cooker to chair to wall to door-to-door handle, just to assure himself that he was hearing things.

Then he thought, "Could it be her? No, she doesn't know where I live. Perhaps she found out from the Students Union? Do they know where I live?" Another thud, inches from his chest. But wasn't this a very male type of thud? Yes. It was definitely a male thud. Had it not been for the protection of the door this "thud's" force would have gone straight through him.

His body was shaking more now but not just with cold.

"Um, Yes?"

"Martin, let me in. I just want to talk to you. Come on man, just let me in— a quiet but intensely intelligent voice, deeply powerful with flattened Northern vowels.

"Who is it?"

"Don't you know? Hasn't she told you about me? I find that very surprising. I find that unbelievable."— an increase in volume and a change of tone that deliberately made quite clear the internal viciousness behind it.

"Look I don't know what you're talking about. I think you've got the wrong person…Um, sorry."

The next thud flung the door from its 'hinges smashing Martin hard on the forehead and arms, hurling him backwards into a contorted heap of excruciating pain on the floor.

"I've got the wrong person have I? Then how do I know your name Martin, Martin, Martin? How do I know where you've been? How do I know what you've been doing and how do I know who you've been doing it with? What have you done to Christine?"

The intruders gaunt white face streamed wet and twitched with cold. The mane of lank black hair was speckled with flakes of dying snow. The long black leather coat and black leather trousers glistened like they were sweating and the old white t-shirt, drenched by the midnight, mid-winter elements, clung to a lean, taut torso. He had the type of powerful physique, domineering presence and disconcerting flash of wild in the eyes in common with those who believe themselves to be all-powerful, to be almighty. This young man had made destruction his clinical science.

"You've changed her, you've changed her, you've made her love you. Well, she doesn't love you. She still loves me. Do you hear me Martin, Martin, Martin? She still loves me."

He had Martin by the throat, his knees were buried into his chest nailing him to the floor, immobilising and controlling him with sickening, overwhelming force. He was squeezing the life out of him. Strangling him. Denying him the right to breathe. In sudden eruptions of blind fury, he occasionally shook Martin from side to side pelting his pulsating head against the wall and chair legs, like a child in a tantrum destroying its doll. Martin could feel the veins in his eyes and head popping like minute balloons. The sparse amount of oxygen left for him to desperately struggle for was imbibed with the rank stench of old, stale cider fuming from the manic mouth (only millimetres away from his own purpling lips) which gnashed out expletives, splattering his eyes and face with steaming, raging spittle.

Then suddenly he stopped. He let go of Martin's throat. Martin gulped down the precious air, gagging on it like a man choking on his first sips of water after days wandering through the desert.

Martin's vision was blurred by mists of crimson rising from the broken blood vessels, clouding his numbing pupils. Images took on a surreal, muddied quality—like those seen by infra-red cameras at night. But although the picture may have been suffering from interference, its 'tangible, terrifying reality was all too clear.

Like a panther studying its prey before the kill, the man sat motionless, cross-legged in the middle of the room, his eyes tracing Martin's form like Sonar.

Martin lay as still as he could, trying to breathe again, trying not to shake, trying not to cry, trying to be nothing, trying to be insignificant, praying that the panther might think this simple kill unworthy of him and prowl on to find stronger more challenging game.

The man sat still, as still as a rock, like a statue of Buddha, or in his case the anti-Buddha, for this creature's religion was surely founded upon pure remorseless violence.

Martin was sure he would be killed by him; it was just a matter of when and how.

"Get up, we're going for a walk."

After an hour's trudge through the icy snow and the biting cold they were out of the town and into what seemed to Martin to be miles and miles of whitened wilderness. Martin followed the man as best he could despite his exhaustion, his acute fear and his unbearable pain. Often he fell and expected the man to kill him on the spot. But the man would pick him up yelling "You're not going to die here," and shunt him onwards.

The man seemed to possess super-human strength and ploughed on through driving wind and snow, crossing field after field and hedges and ditches and snow drifted hills as if this were a normal everyday outing for him.

Despite his terror at what would await him at the end of their tortuous journey, Martin stayed as close behind the man as his fading strength would allow. Firstly, so as not to arouse any great wrath in the man should he drag behind too greatly; but secondly, so as to prolong his life (however physically painful that existence might be) just that little bit longer. He did not want to die. He desperately wanted to live. He would do anything for the man to let him live. But he was too afraid to tell the man that. To beg would be the ultimate act of cowardice in the man's eyes that would kill Martin there and then for sure.

Onward and onward, they strove.

A weak Winter sun rose barely penetrating its mask of silvering, new-born cloud. Barren trees throbbed with heavy snow. No birds heralded this new dawn. There was no sound, barring the crunch, crunch of heavy, tired feet upon the frosted, iced-cold snow.

"Right then, this is it, Martin, Martin, Martin, we're here."

"Where?"

They appeared to be in a huge snow-drifted ditch, that stretched onward into the distant blank.

"Dig."

"What?"

"Get on your hands and knees and dig. Just here."

The man started him off with a crushing heal, smashing the top layer of frozen snow, indicating exactly where "just here" was.

Desperate tears involuntarily flooded Martin's face as his quivering hands pulled at the stubborn snow. He had only two questions left. Two questions for the rest of his life. Would he bury him alive or kill him first?

After two feet of snow, he hit the ground. As he cleared more and more the shining metal of railway tracks became visible.

"Martin, Martin, Martin, you are now standing upon a piece of history. Oh, sorry I should say future-history."

The man jumped into the hole with Martin

"This is the spot, the exact spot where Christine will land. It sounds pretty comical, doesn't it? She's going to "fall" from a train Martin, Martin, Martin, and land exactly where you're standing. Um, she'll die of course. Well, I'll see you Martin, Martin, Martin."

Chapter 6

Some dreams are real. They can be called visions, premonitions, second sight, whatever; the thing that separates real dreams from any other is that these real dreams always come true. And you never forget a real dream, not for the rest of your life you don't.

When he awoke the next morning Martin knew all of these things. As if he had digested a new rule book, Martin's whole perception of life and to a great extent his actual personality had changed in order to accommodate the terrible burden of helpless responsibility heaped upon those who have seen what the future will bring.

But was he completely helpless? Could he somehow warn Christine and change the course of what the Man had called "future history"?

As he shivered in the freezing bedsit early that next morning, he saw another terrifying piece of future history. He would never be able to escape the Man. And the Man would take many forms and relentlessly pursue him, thrusting Martin's face into the burning sun of truth, of future history, whether he wanted to see it or not. Martin had no choice but to accept the fact that the Man for some reason had chosen him to "see". And that whatever he chose to show Martin would automatically become the future. And the Man would sit smugly, the "anti-Buddha" and smile and chuckle, as Martin would scream and scream and tear himself to pieces, as their visions passed into fact; into history. Martin had been chosen as the Man's unwilling accomplice. The Man was bent upon destruction and he was going to start with Christine.

"Helpless", "helpless". Could such a powerful enemy ever be stopped? Perhaps only if Martin never dreamt again? Never slept again? But then could the Man be escaped in death? After all, where had he come from in the first place? And would Martin's death release Christine from the future that the Man had planned for her? Or, once Martin had gone, would he simply choose somebody else to be his "instrument" and kill her anyway?

There had to be a way of changing future history. Martin would have to find the way. In the meantime, he would have to make Christine safe, which meant keeping her away from any potential meetings with him.

Supposing the Man could take any form, possess anybody he wished? If that were true, it actually meant keeping Christine away from everyone until he could vanquish the Man forever. Ultimate caution had to be observed at all times in order to prolong Christine's life.

"After all," Martin said out loud to himself, "they do say that the Devil is a charming man." Therefore, the only person with whom Christine could be guaranteed of safety, would be with the one person who knew her destiny. So, logically, Martin had no choice but to keep by her side at all times and to remove her from the danger of others for as long as that danger existed. How long would the danger continue to exist? — probably for as long as Christine did.

He would have to act quickly. He would have to find Christine and convince her of the danger she was facing. He would have to convince her to hide away with him, to keep away from the others. Then he would explain everything to her: the vision, the Man, the train, everything. She would then understand and she would be grateful. What if she didn't believe him? What if she wouldn't go with him? She would just have to—that was all. She would just have to.

Before leaving the bedsit, Martin opened the single drawer under the one ringed cooker. He took out the one sharp carving knife. He put the knife into the inside pocket of his overcoat and left.

Chapter 7

Progress along the two miles or so that stood between Martin's bedsit and the University was rendered slow and treacherous by the black ice that had formed on the pavements after last night's surprise blizzard. Where, on the roads the night before, there had been feet of snow, now bubbling rivers of muddy slush pervaded, drenching Martin's legs as it sluiced the pavements with every passing vehicle.

An evil, biting wind made sterling attempts to maintain last night's desertion of the streets. The small bands of people that were braving the bleak weather were huddled together in tight groups like poor Russians waiting for loaves of bread.

As he walked and slid and stumbled along, he thought again and again of Christine's mysterious departure and became more and more convinced that the Man had in some way already 'introduced' himself to her; that she somehow knew the danger she was in and had made good her escape from the pub after perhaps sensing the impending arrival of the Man. Why would the Beast claim he loved her and then unleash his unrequited revenge upon her, had he not invaded Christine's dreams and been rejected by her?

Oh, he was a shrewd one. The ultimate hunter. Unable to be seen or touched he marched through the world of the subconscious unchecked and unchallenged, picking off his victims at their most vulnerable—whilst they stumbled through the blackened mass of his world. The world of sleep. The world of dreams.

As Martin rounded the next bend, over the other side of the road, he was surprised to see a very ordinary looking small Catholic church. The surprise being that he had never noticed the church before. Martin had never been religious, so perhaps churches were automatically edited from his mind whenever he'd come across one. Previously the Church, or religion had not occupied a thought or cell in his body. However, the events of the previous night had made him now seriously consider that the Devil, at least, might have a place in some form of reality. Certainly whatever, or whoever it was that he had "experienced" could not possibly be "of this world" although the tangibility of the Man's terrible intent was as clear and as real to him as was the plain stone building before him.

Did Martin now feel the need, for the first time in his life, to be blessed, or protected by 'God's love'? Or did he hope that the Man could not penetrate the sanctity of its walls and that he could safely think for a moment? If the Man could read Martin's thoughts and knew his every move, perhaps their transmission might be blocked by the holy walls? Perhaps, inside a church, the Man would not be able to 'hear'?

Martin pushed open the reassuringly heavy outer door and quietly slid onto a pew in a murky corner at the back of the church.

He was an alien in an alien land.

His senses were bombarded with the ancient and the holy. His eyes had to adjust themselves to the dim candlelight, shrouded in plumes of incense. Shadowed walls with dark oak hide-aways whispered secret sins and the slight rattle of rosary beads in the shaking, arthritic hands of an old Italian lady, veiled and in black, added authenticity to the clichés that he suspected he'd find beyond the heavy outer door.

Considering that it was relatively early in the morning the twenty or so people that were sitting in the church were twenty or so more people than he had imagined there would be. Upon further inspection, though, he noticed a uniformed shabbiness to the clothes of the majority and he concluded that these were some of the city's homeless, grasping a few hours respite from the Arctic conditions outside.

A confessor snuck away from the "whispering wall" and knelt before the altar. How many "hail Mary's"? How many "fruits of thy womb?" The temptation for Martin to burst out laughing due to sheer amazed excitement at actually witnessing a religious ritual hitherto consigned to myth or "Godfather" films, was almost uncontrollable. However, his sense of respect and propriety prevailed and, re-gaining control of himself, he managed to maintain his silent privileged position of inconspicuous observer at the back of the church.

The old Italian lady a few pews ahead of him made her weary way to the confessional.

Martin wondered what she must have looked like when she was young. Was she beautiful? "Time is cruel" he said to himself. Had she always believed? Had she always gone to confession? Or was it only recently, scared by the approach of inevitable death that she had sought to cleanse her soul? There was an enviable sense of 'belonging' with her, like she had had the comfort all of her life of being part of a large, exclusive, protective club.

Did the Man bother trying to infiltrate the minds of staunch believers? Were they protected from him by 'God's love'? Was it only the weak, unsure, non-believers that he targeted as vessels condemned to carry his cargo of destruction?

If the Man was the Devil, or a disciple, could Martin then conversely accept the existence of God? And if these buildings of bricks and mortar (that had previously seemed to Martin merely to represent "graven images of the Lord thy God"— and to have been erected as nothing more than a meeting point for scared mortal men and women to exorcise that universal human foible, the progressive strain of impending death— and to self-satisfactorily answer the mystery of "where we go" by granting themselves immortality in their Heaven with their God)—if they really were the houses of God, then could the man granting absolutions to those entering the confessional truly be a conduit to God?

If it were all true. If it were all true. If the Priest could contact God. Then could not Martin contact God via him and let God know that the Beast was abroad, plundering the subconscious mind, evading detection?

The Man was real. The threat to Christine was real. The old lady with her rosary beads and her belief was real. Was God real? It was time to find out.

The old lady left the confessional and knelt before the altar. An old man shivered a few isles down from Martin and then descended again into sleep. All was still. The church flickered with candlelight. Saints raised and lowered their heads as the stained glasses glowed in tandem with the shimmering light.

Martin stood nervously, as if about to read aloud a piece from the Bible to the rest of a school's assembly, he reticently approached the front of the church. He felt the stares from the tiny crowd. As if he were an under-cover cop wishing to avoid detection, he lit a candle at a small shrine on his way hoping that this was the right thing to do. He reached the door to the confessional. Like a businessman entering a Soho bookshop, he involuntarily looked around to check that he wasn't being observed. All eyes were upon him. He paused for a moment, opened the small, panelled oak door, and went into the confessional.

Inside the darkened closet all was silent. Martin could smell the Priest's cheap aftershave. He began to feel claustrophobic. Despite the latticed screen that separated them, Martin felt uncomfortably close to the Priest.

"How long has it been since your last confession?"

The quiet, well-spoken voice sounded as bored as it did ritualistic. Childish excitement gripped Martin. He was trespassing in a neighbour's garden.

"Can you talk to God?"

Martin heard the Priest's chair creek as he shuffled uncomfortably.

"Well, well sometimes my payers are answered, but I thought you came here to con—"

"Good, good. I'm going to tell you what I know and then you can tell him."

"All right."

"He's here among us, the Man, I mean, the Devil."

"Where exactly is he?"

"Well, he's in my head at the moment um, last night when I was asleep I dreamt about him but the dream was real. He told me what he was going to do to Christine, he's going to hurt her, he's going to…well, I don't know how to stop him. You see, whatever I dream while he's there showing me, whatever it is — it will come true do you see? It's the future history, it always comes true. And he has predicted that Christine will die and she will, she will unless I can find a way of changing the vision, of altering the future. The only way I can think of doing that is by removing her from the places of danger. I mean the others. You see he himself, he won't do the killing, oh no, he won't ever show himself enough for that.

"He'll get someone else to do it. He lives in our dreams and he can see into whichever future he wishes. So, if he saw a future for someone where they killed her, then they would have to, because it's their future. I mean what choice would they have. It's very clever isn't it. I mean it's bloody simple but it's clever isn't it. Murder without ever murdering. It's, it's all mighty. That's why I have to get Christine away from everyone. We won't ever know who it is when he or she comes, so the best policy is to keep her in isolation until it's over. That's why I'm here you see. I thought you'd better tell God and then he could banish him or be rid of him or something and Christine and I could be safe again."

The chair creaked again, and for a long while the Priest said nothing. Then he spoke in a studied, measured tone that sounded as if he had the lines already memorised, it had merely taken him a while to remember the correct text.

"We all have the Devil within us. We are all capable of succumbing to evil. It is up to each of us to take responsibility for our own actions."

"But you don't understand, he doesn't give you that option . He controls them from within. It's only me he's given a sporting chance to because I was too easy game last night. He wants to watch me try to save her. He thinks it's impossible, but it amuses him to see me try. Look I've never been to a church before, I don't even know if I believe in God, but you do. You'd have a chance to warn God. He wouldn't expect that. I'm sure one of the reasons he chose me was because I'm a long way from God. He thinks I'm isolated and alone. This could release Christine. Just tell him."

"What are you planning on doing to Christine?"

"Me, me? Well, I'm planning on saving her life, aren't I? I mean, isn't that what I've just been bloody saying?"

"All right, then how do you plan to keep her in isolation? And what if she doesn't want to be kept?"

"Well she will once I've explained it to her, but I've got to get her away quickly. So, if she doesn't understand me or believe me at first, at least, once I've got her away, I'll know she's safe while I explain the whole bloody thing to her. Which, incidentally, I hope doesn't take as long to get through as it's bloody doing with you."

"You're going to kidnap an innocent girl. What are you going to do to her when you've—"

"I'm going to bloody well save her life you stupid bastard!"

Martin flew out of the confessional and hurried towards the back of the church and freedom.

214

"Stop him, stop him. Listen to me you must not go through with this—"

Martin burst into a run, scurrying toward the door. Simultaneously, a group of four of the homeless men arrived in front of the door and slowly, tentatively began to advance on Martin. He could feel the pungent presence of the hateful Priest behind him. He reached into his coat and brandished the carving knife for them all to see. The men in front dispersed but the Priest would not leave.

"Listen to me my son, you—"

Martin slashed backhanded across the Priests 'cheek. The flash of silver was laced with threads of red as his cheek gaped like a sliced melon. Blood spewed from the Priests face. He was trying to hold the slashed cheek together but his hands slipped repeatedly upon the virgin blood ejaculating from the writhing mass like a fountain. The old Italian lady began to wail and offer up prayers in her native tongue. The others stared in frightened astonishment. The sanctity of their church had been destroyed.

"You're a fool Priest. He's here, he's here and he'll get you all." Martin fumbled with the latch to the heavy door. Turning back, he saw them helping the Priest to his feet, whose face, hands and hair were steeped in gouts of fresh blood.

Now they had no option. Martin and Christine would now have to disappear for ever.

Dashing out of the church Martin collided with a young woman who screamed and slipped and fell hard onto the ice. She focused upon the dripping knife that was still in his hand.

In desperate panic she began to sob: "Please, please don't hurt me, please…"

He slithered the bloodied weapon into his inside coat pocket.

He ran as best he could away from the church, away from the frightened girl, and, away from God.

Chapter 8

By the time Martin had reached "their" pub it was half past eleven and the blonde barmaid was just re-opening its 'doors.

"Oh, hello love, can't keep you away can we. Did you 'ave any luck love? Did yu 'find her?"

Martin silently pushed passed the barmaid and made his way to the deserted bar.

"Well I think yu'r better off without her love, I mean how strange can yu 'get, eh? Eh, are you all right love you look like you've been up all night, yu 'look 'arf froze, yu'll catch yu ' death yu 'know."

"Um, lager, could I have a pint of lager please?"

Martin stood at the bar in abandoned shock. He was attempting, in his mind, to recreate what had happened— trying to picture what he had done to the Priest.

Was this him? It couldn't be him. He was shy. He was kind. He would never, could never hurt anyone. And yet there he stood, alone and guilty. By now the police were bound to be on his trail. Pursuing a violent madman.

"It's not me," he whispered to himself.

The barmaid brought him his pint.

Since being in the church, and now, in the bar, Martin had had the surreal urge to stop and to drink and drink and drink. He still could not picture, with any real clarity, exactly what he had just done. He knew that he had done something beyond his personality, something horrific. Yet the need to quench his thirst for alcohol strangely took prominence in his head. His mouth dried like sand at the thought of drink, and only drink could re-moisten it.

He ordered his second pint.

As he paid, he saw the barmaid notice his bloodied hand.

"Oh, I was changing a wheel for somebody," he lied "my hand slipped."

"Oh," (she didn't believe him), "not been 'aving much luck lately have yu 'love."

"No."

For some reason Martin trusted in the barmaid's "total discretion assured" tone. Like a prostitute, it would have been disruptive to her business not to have turned a deaf ear, or to have gone around "telling tales" whenever she came across "strange" things. She wore upon her face the constant experienced expression of, "well, it takes all sorts". He felt assured that (as long as he had the money) she would allow him to escape into the "liquid amber" without ever raising a judgmental eyebrow.

He ordered his third pint.

"Hello Jack. The usual?"

An old local had silently entered the familiarity of "his" pub and sat at his usual table waiting for his "usual".

"There you are my love," she gave Martin his pint.

"What do you fancy in the three thirty at Doncaster then Jack?"

"Lady Summersby," was the gruff emphatic reply.

As the alcohol warmed him, Martin began to feel strangely "local" himself. He looked across to Jack trying to catch his aged eye beneath the cloth cap. Beyond him Martin could see the ladies toilets. Last night's scene with Christine re-enacted itself. He felt his presence to be conspicuously ghostly by her absence. This was their pub. What had happened to her? He knew that he had to find her, but he needed more time to think. More time to drink. He sat at Jack's table. The gnarled hands were in the steady process of making their well-rehearsed roll-up. Martin's limbs began to feel heavy with drink. He plonked his pint down on Jack's table and spilled some. Jack looked up briefly and then continued to manufacture his cigarette.

"Well, what's happened to the weather then Jack?"

The dry lips parted as he licked the cigarette paper.

"They promised it'ud be bad. Best off indoors." Jack took a studied sip of his stout, and then lit his cigarette.

"Um, well, do you reckon it's here to stay?"

"Could be."

The grumpy old man's ritual was being broken. He never spoke to anyone. Just a quiet pint with his fag. He took out a rolled-up copy of The Sun from his overcoat pocket and, thumbing the page three girl as he went, he turned his back on Martin.

Martin got the message and returned to the bar.

The barmaid was cleaning glasses and took a few minutes to notice Martin nodding towards his now empty pint glass.

"Same again is it love?"

"Yes please."

As he waited for his pint the pub began to refill with a lunchtime crowd of students flush with new grant cheques and intent upon squandering them as quickly and as drunkenly as possible.

"Thanks love," she said.

He carefully gulped at his new pint.

The group of students were typically over friendly with each other, over confident and over loud. Grumpy Jack was shaking his head and mumbling curses at the rowdy group that had invaded his pub.

Sitting on a tall bar stool at the bar, Martin felt himself to be swaying as if in a gentle breeze. His taste for the lager was becoming more insatiable with every swig. The delicious fizz hit the back of his throat as the flavourful bubbles burst; and the potent liquid dulled his mind sufficiently to give him a brief, if albeit artificial pause. He had reached that plateau of drunkenness in which the most experienced drinker knows to remain silent and passive and to observe others' ridiculous behaviour before behaving that way himself.

Martin's foot slipped off the rung of his bar stool. He lost his balance and spilled some of his drink whilst steadying himself upon the now sodden bar. The barmaid arrived with her cloth, expertly assessed his state and decided he'd be good for a few quid more.

Whilst watching Martin drain his existing pint, the barmaid simultaneously placed a fresh one on the table and took his moist five-pound note with a knowing, flirtatious grin. She handed him his change and he dropped a ten pence piece onto the floor whilst putting the money into his trouser pocket. The disobedient coin defiantly rolled towards "Grumpy Jack" and nestled itself under Grumpy's highly polished Hush Puppy.

"Excuse me Jack.., excuse me Jack, but I think my 10p is under, um, is under your shoe."

"Oh, is it now?" He lifted his foot revealing the coin. "Yes now, there it is. I wandered what had happened to that 10p, very attached to that I was" and he picked up the coin and put it in the breast pocket of his tweed sports jacket and went back to the page three girl.

Martin blinked in stunned incredulity.

"Jack, come on Jack me old mate, don't muck around. Give me my ten pence, please."

"I am not your mate and I never muck around."

His eyes did not waver from the newspaper and the breasts of "curvy Karen from Coventry"!

Martin snatched the newspaper from the old man's hands.

"Give me my fucking ten pence you arrogant old bastard."

"All right son, all right I was only mucking you around."

He placed the coin on the table and looked Martin full in the face for the first time. Martin recognised genuine fear in the old man's eyes.

The fracas, such as it was, lasted for mere seconds and, luckily for Martin, went largely unnoticed by the rest of the pub. Except of course for the barmaid who surprisingly gave Martin a reassuring smile and added with familiar sarcasm, "You being an 'orrible old buzzard again Jack. You want to watch yourself, else one day someone'll give you a bloody good hiding" adding under her breath "and they can have a drink on me if they do!"

Martin moved to a barstool as far away from Jack as was possible. He was shaking.

He bought another pint of lager and drunk the first half down in one. The drink was now taking its 'toll and he slumped over

221

the bar, his head in his hands. Haunting images of the Man faded in and out of his head as he went over and over what he had done to the Priest. He began to feel sick at the thought of all the blood. Blood was everywhere in his mind. He remembered Christine's laughter and her hair and her smell. But the Man invaded his head and took hold of Christine. She was screaming.

She was on a train. The door to the train opened. She screamed. She fell from the train her body twisting and rolling along the track in a hideous haze of ever-increasing red. As the noise from the train subsided into the distance it was replaced by the crunching of bones upon metal and rock as her spinning body slowed to a contorted stop. Blood was everywhere in his head. Her twisted body lay in a lifeless, gory heap upon the track. Blood was everywhere…

His half-filled pint glass smashing upon the floor "awoke" him. He looked around the hushed pub but couldn't focus on anything.

"Are you all right love?" the barmaid was now less than sympathetic.

"Yes, um,. yes …could you, could you tell me where the toilet is please?"

She came around to his side of the bar, dustpan and brush in hand, and physically "pointed" him in the right direction.

"Thank you."

He staggered off leaning on chairs and tables as he went. He saw "Grumpy Jack" looking at him, tutting and shaking his head.

In the ammonia smelling "gents" he leaned upon the wash basin and tried to focus upon his face in the cracked mirror. He saw little specks of dried blood on his nose and cheeks. He desperately scrubbed his face with the ice-cold water. As he looked again into the mirror at his sopping face, heat began to rise from his alcohol filled, raging guts. He dashed into the cubicle and was violently sick.

Leaving the gents toilet, he could taste stale apples in his mouth. It was the same "taste" that he had smelled upon the Man's breath.

"I'll never escape him," he thought to himself as he sat on his stool. "He has possessed me."

The vomiting had made him feel slightly more sober, so he got the attention of the barmaid.

"Don't you think you've 'ad enough love?"

"No, no, it's okay, I'll just have one more."

"Well as long as it is only one. And try to get it in your mouth this time!" She poured him his pint with her "it takes all sorts" expression on.

"Grumpy Jack" got up, folded his newspaper, put it into his overcoat pocket, placed his empty glass upon the bar and left without speaking.

Martin slammed the liquid down his throat and resurrected the comfortable out of focus haze.

He thanked the barmaid, carefully removed himself from the stool and staggered out of the pub.

Like a vampire in need of blood, he stalked the streets hunting for another pub to have more drink. He had the "taste" for it now. His dried mouth was in desperate need of "lubrication".

It didn't take him too long to come across the next pub. He did not notice its name, nor did he take in any of the blurred lunchtime faces, nor any features of the furniture or the bar. All he looked at was the barman and the glass that he filled for him. He took his pint over to a small table by the window and watched life go by.

On the other side of the road was a petite French restaurant. It had an "oldie worldie" sign over its 'door "Le Tire Bouchon" and was decorated in dark greens with a lot of hanging baskets and plants inside and out. At the table in the window of the restaurant was a girl with long brown hair. Although she was sitting with her back to the window Martin knew, or sensed immediately, that she was Christine.

She was with a young man of about twenty years old. He was sitting opposite Christine. Martin had a very detailed view of him. The smart grey suit, the slick blonde hair, the oh so charming smile. Everything about him was confident and sophisticated. Martin swigged his pint. He felt fury rising within him, twisted with jealousy, envy and betrayal. "So this must be the "cool" boyfriend I suppose." (He took a bigger gulp of beer). Or was he one of His disciples? Had the Man got to work already, enticing Christine away from Martin in order to destroy her? Martin had no choice.

He would have to keep her in his sights and when the right moment came, he would remove her from his grasp. The waitress came to their table to take their orders. Martin saw Christine throw her head back, laughing that delicious laugh, as she "lucky dip style" pointed her finger down onto the menu. There was more laughter from the "disciple" and the waitress. The waitress left. The boy had love in his eyes for Christine, Martin could see that. What a clever ploy! If only Martin could see her face, then he could tell whether or not she was being taken in. He felt angry with her. Why did she leave him? Why did she leave him?

As they were at the beginning of their meal Martin felt that it would be safe enough to leave her there for a few moments while he got himself another pint.

Back at his table he avidly watched them. Starter, main course, desert, coffee. The "disciple" paid the bill and they left the restaurant. Martin followed a short distance behind them. Shop after shop after street after street he followed, an undetected shadow. Eventually they reached a small terraced house in a street not dissimilar to his own. They went inside holding hands and shut the door behind them.

Martin decided to wait until nightfall.

Chapter 9

It was about four o'clock when the light began to fade on that desolate, cold Winter's afternoon. The effects of the alcohol and the cold sent Martin into bouts of "waking" sleep in which, as he drifted in and out of dreams, the Man-made numerous appearances manifesting himself as hideous mask-like faces in various poses of silent hilarious laughter.

Martin would jump up and walk around, rubbing his numb fingers against his face in an attempt to remain fully awake and in this "World". He would then sit down on the garden wall opposite the house that Christine had gone into with the "disciple" earlier that afternoon, and continue his lonely, frozen surveillance.

So far, during his three-hour vigil, there had been no movement or signs of life in either of the two downstairs bay windows, nor the upstairs bedroom windows, which had had their curtains drawn.

A combination of fear, jealousy, rage and envy erupted within him as his imagination introduced to him scenes of sex between the "disciple" and Christine; torturing his flagging and confused mind. The thing that kept him reasonably sane was the knowledge that the "disciple" could not kill her here. She had to fall from a train at the exact spot, along the very length of track that the Man had shown him the night before. And so, he could risk the time and endure the thought of them together in the knowledge that Christine was relatively safe and that he could wait until they were asleep, when the "disciple" would be unable to defend himself... Once he had been dealt with, Martin could then explain everything to Christine and they could disappear together.

Of course, Martin had anticipated that Christine might not believe him, or that she may not have seen through the disciple's cunning overtures and have grown attached to him. Whatever her reaction, he would have no choice but to force her to come with him, to be out of sight of the others, out of the Man's reach.

As each hour passed the effects of the alcohol waned until the sober truth of what Martin had done in the church, and the true gravity of his present situation, and the potential repercussions of what he was about to do, slashed Martin's resolve into frightened shreds. The harsh, clear diamond of reality had cut its way through the alcoholic fug of ignorant optimism and was compelling him to turn away and to run. Should he give himself up to the police? Assault on a priest with a deadly weapon would hardly make him a candidate for early parole. Besides, if Martin knew anything he knew that he would never survive prison.

The only option was for him to run. To leave the Country. And run.

However, the reality of the dreams and of the Man had more potent authenticity, had more of a ghastly sense of absolute reality than the most severe truth that could be served up in this World. And the consequences of abandoning Christine to Him far outweighed anything that the mortal men and women of Earth could possibly do to him. Besides, would the Man ever really let him escape? Even if he could get away physically, the net result would be that He would kill Christine and then chastise and pursue Martin with the images of her death for the rest of his life.

He would have stay and fight it out. With Christine by his side, they would live or die together.

All of the lights were off in the house.

It was now one o'clock in the morning.

Whether the disciple was asleep or not it was now time to remove Christine from the Man's clutches. If that meant killing the disciple then he would.

He took the knife out of his pocket, a car's headlights sluiced by and he saw bobbles of dried blood upon the blade.

He prised open one of the bay windows with the knife, it was surprisingly easy to do.

The house was almost completely bare, obviously she had just moved in. No furniture for him to avoid cluttering over in the dark. The house was in silence. They were asleep. He carefully climbed the stairs. He gently opened the door of the first bedroom he came to and peered in. A street lamp just outside filtered through the curtains gently illuminating the unmistakable curves of the female form beneath the blankets. She was on her own! She hadn't slept with him. She must have seen through him. So, where was he?

The room next to Christine's was not so well illuminated, it being that much further away from the street lamp, but even so, Martin could make him out, breathing heavily under the bedclothes. Martin's arm shook violently as he stoically attempted to hold the knife firmly enough by the handle.

Chapter 10

That's the sun. Yes, it is. I can feel it warming my back. But surely, I've forgotten, or evaporated too much to feel things or to care?

There's sand in my hand and under my fingernails, itching me. I turn over and open my eyes and I'm blinded by a hot sun.

I sneeze.

As my pupils adjust themselves to the light, I can see a calm red sea only yards from me. A little wave laboriously gathers momentum, speeds towards me, pauses for a moment, and then changes its mind.

I look around me, the beach is deserted. There isn't a clump of grass, or a bird, or anything other than the white sand, brown pebbles and me. It's all so very uninterrupted. Even the sea seems "turned down" making its sojourns to the shore in a reverential hush. I am alone. All alone. Is this heaven? Why am I alone? Suddenly, along the distant shoreline, I make out two tiny faint figures. Are they coming towards me? But just as suddenly as they had appeared I lose them again in the distant yellow haze.

"No!"

I start to run along the shore, my feet occasionally slipping on the shiny pebbles. I try to stay on the hard wet sand, but the terrain seems to change with every step and my going is slow, too slow. I stop and look around me. They are nowhere. I'm alone. "Oh God what have I done? I'm in Hell, I'm in Hell."

I crash onto the sand; it sticks to my wet knees. I would cry but my despair is too great. I just sit there. What else can I do?

"What's your name?"

A blonde little girl in a white swimsuit is standing next to me.

"Christine."

"Christine, Christine…you were right mummy!"

I turn and standing behind me is a beautiful blond woman in her own version of the child's white swimsuit.

"I, I don't believe this. I've seen you both before. You were in the magazine, on the train."

Chapter 11

As Martin stealthily approached the sleeping Disciple in his bed, the room began to pulsate with the faded blue flashing of a police car in the street below. It had stopped directly outside Christine's house. How could they know so quickly? A description? Going in the same direction that he took from the church? The barmaid? Of course, the barmaid. She would have described Christine to them from the night before and — He heard a man talking on a radio, and another saying that he thought that they had the right address. Martin froze, staring at the window, listening. He would have to do it now or not at all. He gripped the knife and returned his panicked attention to the sleeping Disciple. But to his amazement, the extra light (albeit it filtered through the closed curtains) revealed to Martin not the enemy that he was preparing to kill, but a rather large, cuddly yellow Labrador snoring soundly upon the bed.

He heard Christine wake with a frightened start. She called for "Sam". The yellow Lab awoke, pricked up its ears and sniffed around Martin's sodden legs.

Christine called him again and he dutifully lumbered off into Christine's room. He heard her get out of bed. She turned the hall light on. From the shadows of the spare room, he saw Christine. She stood on the landing, shaking at the top of the stairs; holding onto the dog's collar, listening intently to the activity outside. She was in her nightie and a thick old green woollen jumper, her legs were bare, she had blue socks on her feet. She sat on the top stair and hugged her dog. She was very scared.

Finally, a knock at the front door made her body quake. Sam let out a single, unconvincing bark followed by manic licking of Christine's face as if he wanted to be praised for his bravery. Martin was only a matter of feet away from her. Spare strands of her tousled "bedly" hair stood up towards the landing's single light bulb. He crept back into the deep blue shadows. As if sensing his presence Christine suddenly turned and peered into the murk of the spare room. Martin thought that she had seen him, it looked as though she was staring straight at him and he was about to leave his hiding place and give himself up to her, when she turned and descended the stairs keeping Sam close by her side by holding on tightly to his collar.

Martin sat on the bed. He heard the door open and two men talking in hushed voices. Every now and then a walkie talkie would beep and one of them would respond to it. He heard Christine speak although he could not make out what she was saying.

The two men walked away and the front door closed.

Martin walked out of the spare room and stood at the top of the stairs. Christine was still at the front door, leaning against it as if she had lost the power to move, with her back to Martin. Sam spotted Martin and let out a single bark and began to wag his tail excitedly.

"Oh, Sam shut up." She turned from the door and then fell back against it in shock at seeing Martin standing at the top of her staircase. For a while she stood in petrified, motionless, fear: staring at him as if he were an illusion or a ghost.

Then her eyes started to twitch and to trace his body, eventually settling upon the bloodied knife that was still in his hand. There was an unreal silence. Christine let out a terrified, heart-quaking scream as she frantically turned and struggled with the lock on the front door in an attempt to escape. Martin flew down the stairs.

"No, please no. I'm here to help." He pushed her away from the door.

She ran into the kitchen and desperately scurried through the kitchen drawers. She found a long bread knife and pointed it out at Martin, holding it in both of her trembling hands, as she tearfully backed away from him until she was up against the cooker and could go no further.

"Please get away from me, please don't hurt me," she sobbed.

Sam ran between the two of them in confused excitement, knocking the kitchen chairs as he went, as if he thought this all to be of great fun and excitement.

"I don't know why you've done what you've done, I don't know why the Police say that you were talking about me? Is it because of yesterday? Look I'm really sorry. I had to pick someone up from the station, I thought it would only take me two minutes. The pub was so crowded, I couldn't get to you at the bar so I got off to deal with it all as quickly as I could. Look, I'm such a scatter-brain. But there was all that snow and my car wouldn't start and I had to wait for the A.A. and Oh, God, I can tell you don't believe me but it's the truth. Please, look we can go out again and I promise I won't go anywhere, yes, we'll go for a nice drink, we'll get soundly pissed just the two of us. Just please, please don't hurt me. Please don't kill me."

She was crying and pleading as you would if you were being dragged towards the executioner's axe.

Then, as suddenly as the fear had gripped her it strangely disappeared, and she seemed resigned to her fate. She believed that she was going to die. Martin saw the frantic struggle for life vanish from her eyes as she stooped against the cooker in limp submission. For the second time that day Martin felt sick.

He gently placed his knife onto the small Formica-topped kitchen table, the handle towards Christine. "Where's the D—, um where's your boyfriend?" he asked in a whisper.

Christine began to laugh exhaustedly, "He's not my boyfriend, he's my little cousin Richard, and he's gone back home. That's who I went to pick up last night. He had an interview at the university this morning, not that he probably felt so hot after having to wait hours for me last night in the freezing cold."

Martin sat down at the table and stared at the knife.

"Martin, what's happened to you? Why did you hurt the Priest? The Police are looking everywhere for you. They said that you kept on talking about, about me to the Priest. Why? What is it Martin? I don't believe you meant to hurt anyone did you?"

Martin's acute exhaustion was returning and his head began to nod in time with his pounding heart.

"No, I didn't."

"Well, what is it then? Christ, I can't believe you wanted to kidnap me! I mean what have I done to you? You don't even know me. You know the Police are going up and down this street right now. Just waiting for you to arrive. One shout from me and they'll—

"I love you Christine. I, I'm sorry if I've frightened you… I didn't mean to hurt that Priest but he was going to stop me, and nothing must get in my way. I love you Christine, but he wants you dead, I can't let that happen."

There was an awful believability to Martin's half waking speech that stunned Christine. She sat opposite him at the table. She placed her knife on top of the shiny work surface, but she still kept the handle pointing in her direction.

They sat in silence for what must have been two or three minutes. To them, after the manic events of that night it must have seemed like two hours.

Finally, Christine spoke. "Who wants to kill me Martin?"

But fatigue had beaten him and he sat at the table and slept.

The logical thing to do would have been to slip off quietly and to call the Police. They would take him away and he would be out of her life forever. But as he sat there, gently snoring, he looked like a homeless child in need of a safe place to lay his head, away from the dangers of the street and she felt pity for the lonely outcast boy who was afraid of everyone. And besides, the feelings that she had felt for him the night before were real. She really did like him, despite what he had done.

Indeed, in a strange, almost perverse way, the thought of him being wanted by the Police excited her, as if she were harbouring William Bonnie under her roof. Could he be telling the truth, or was he just scared? Jealous? Mad? Good reason enough for not turning him into the Police was that she feared that he could possibly be telling some kind of strange, cruel truth. Could there really be someone out there who wanted her dead?

She put his arm over her shoulder and "sleep-walked" him up the stairs. She was struck by how thin and frail and light he was. She pulled back her covers and slid his wasted form under them. She felt more as if she were putting a 10-year-old to bed, rather than a wanted dangerous fugitive. She sat on the bed next to him. She observed the damp black hair, the gaunt, pale, twitching face and the still trembling hand on top of the covers. For a long while she sat and looked, her expressionless face absorbing every feature of his, as he lay there at her mercy. Until eventually, as if deliberately defying all logic like some kind of gentle dare-devil; or as if she had reached a definite conclusion about him, she softened and she smiled.

Martin's eyes gradually opened. Pain singed his eyeballs from his brain outwards. He was surprisingly hot in the freezing bedroom, cloaked in the deep, blue-black night. Only his eyelids moved, the rest of his body remained motionless, suspended as if in paralysis. As soon as he took that first blink, the rest of his numbed senses awoke and, as if he had been aroused from a deep coma, all was new and glorious and wondrous on that cold, still, Winter's night. For the second time in twenty-four hours, he was filled with "her". Her "essence" flowed into, devoured and conquered every cell in his disbelieving mind. He was lying with her, in her bed, inches from her parted, sleeping lips, his body hot, almost sweating from the tender warmth generated by hers.

Although they were not quite touching, their closeness under the old duvet, the outer side of which was chilled by the freezing bedroom air, generated the sensations of that privileged proximity felt from a first tender kiss between lovers. He dare not move, dare not shatter the illusion that he was indeed in bed with his girlfriend, his wife, the woman that he would love for all time; he dare not lose this moment, this unbelievable moment with the goddess, with Helen; he dare not do anything that might disturb her and prompt her to wake up. He lay motionless, in a stillness like suspended animation. He barely dared to breathe. Their lips were almost touching. He was breathing in her carbon dioxide. The street lamp outside the window created a soft orange beam through the gauze curtains that picked out each individual eyelash, each line of her eyelids, each movement of her eyes beneath.

She moved. Her arm flopped heavily upon his waist. Unbeknown to her she was holding him. Suddenly her eyes opened and she looked straight at him, her pupils millimetres from his. She did not pull away, react, or even blink. Her giant eyes stared into his.

"It's so cold, isn't it Martin."

"Yes."

"Are you okay?"

"Yes."

Her eyes flicked down to the arm that was still looped around his waist. She looked back into his child's eyes. She did not move her arm. Nor did she blink, nor do anything that might denote embarrassment or a surreptitious wish to move her arm. Again, they stared, pupil to pupil.

However, we perceive time and use its calibration to compartmentalise the events that count, no such theory would have been of any consequence to them as they lay in that stagnated vortex that we have all experienced but have no name for other than "when time stood still". If the times when "time stands still" cannot exist, then are the events that take place within that bizarre spectrum equally fantastical? One thing was for certain on that strange, strange night; neither of them wanted the reality of stark daybreak to come, ever.

The witching hour had them in its warm, comfortable, abstract clutches. Escape would have been futile. For any prisoner to escape, the initial longing for freedom has to be there. The orange glow of the street lamp seemed to deepen, giving the effect of a mystical, mandarin fog, as if they were the main protagonists in an old, sepia-toned movie. Very gently, moving millimetres of a millimetre, she began minute caresses of his waist. Despite his thick woollen jumper, the tiny movement was so vast in this oblique world of silence and stillness, that Martin almost jumped due to the clamorous din of jumper and blanket against microscopically moving skin.

Martin could taste mint. A sweet warm mint. His senses felt like they were no longer his own, he had never smelled, nor touched, nor heard, nor tasted?—She pulled her lips away from his and she smiled at him. A tiny string of saliva swung from her lip onto his chin. Martin could feel the beginnings of uncontrollable convulsions in his body. His whole being could not accept the possibility that this was real and, as if in angry reaction to some preposterous suggestion, he felt bitterly sad and terribly, terribly wronged. A desperate tear ran the length of Martin's nose and splashed onto the side of hers.

"Martin what's wrong?" Only her lips moved, all the rest of existence was as still as ever.

He looked downwards into the warm bedding with the girl's hand upon his waist.

"I, I love you, but, but I know that in the morning— well, um I know that you could never love me."

"You know, for a geography student you're pretty lost most of the time!"

"What?"

"Look at me, Martin. Look at me."

Martin looked into her shimmering eyes but, as he did, blinding tears flooded from the ducts. With her thumb she gently wiped the salty film from his cheek and softly pulled her fingers through his dank hair as if he were her baby. He looked away again. She took hold of his chin and forced his disbelieving eyes back up to hers. She regarded him with a profound seriousness that he had not seen in her before.

"I don't know what is happening Martin, I don't know how we have ended up here, it's all kind of cloudy to me, but, as we lie here, I will tell you that I love you. And, when you wake up in the morning, I will tell you again."

She kissed him, deeply upon the lips. Everything about her was deep and rich and full of life and love.

When they were naked, they held each other, her head upon his chest and shoulder, her leg curled over his, her arm under his neck, her other hand stroking his hair, her lips kissing his cheek, her hot breath in his ear. And that is how, on that first frozen night, they kept warm and secure. They were not just together; they were as one. So much at one that when they finally did make gentle love, it felt more to them as a continuation of that beautiful sensation of "oneness".

There was no telling where one part of her body stopped or where his began. Neither of them sought anything from the other, nor was there any need to give. When they made love, they simply became a gentle expression of each other, within each other. There could be nothing desperate with them. No sex. Just them. And when they eventually merged with sleep, they were entwined together, like the branches of a wild ancient wood, lying breathless and calm and safe.

Chapter 12

It was the morning cold that woke him, freezing his toes that were sticking out of the end of the bedclothes. The drawn curtains gave the room a dulled but pleasant pallor. Although he did not look out of the window, the atmosphere was one of being snowed in. A kind of womb-like feeling. Only with the increased light of morning could he now see how decrepit the bedroom was. It was virtually bereft of all furniture, save the soft double bed that he now sat up in and a large armchair on which was thrown a massive mound of her clothes.

The brown (probably once cream) wallpaper was peeling away from the walls and around the corners and skirting boards was speckled black dots of mouldy damp. A full-length mirror rested up against the wall in front of him, upon its corners hung two black bras and a red felt hat. He heard a car sluish by outside. He rubbed his eyes and they hurt him. It was a kind of muscular pain around the sockets which he supposed had been caused by forcing them open for too long.

Yet he had slept and the Man had not come. What could this mean? He was sure that He would never ever let him rest. Was it another clever ploy? Or could all of this just have been a dream? A proper dream?

He looked down at the sleeping Christine who was completely submerged under the warm covers except for a mass of anonymous chestnut hair protruding from the top. If it had been a proper dream then Martin was guilty not only of madness but of a terrible, mindless assault upon that poor priest.

The strange thing was though, that even though he now had a very clear picture of all that he had done, he really did not feel any great guilt. And this he could only attribute to the absolute existence of the Man.

He had been there with him, in the snow, on the railway track. It was all real, it had to have been. If he ever thought what had happened was not then he would play into the Man's hands and at that point the Man would surely strike and kill her. Yes, that must have been His plan. He would leave it long enough for Martin to forget, for Martin to become slack and then He would take her from him.

Martin had to remember. Every day he had to recognise the danger even if on the surface of it his love was safe. Did she love him? Really love him? Her body was curved away from him. As he lay down beneath the covers he saw her naked back, the slope of her slender hips. For a time, he secretly peeped at her nakedness, her beauty, the stuff that was forbidden to other men. Why him? Why him? He coyly shuffled as close as he could to her without actually touching her. He wanted to feel her, but feeling the heat from her skin was enough for him, was as far as he could dare go without her being awake and taking the lead. Anyway, he couldn't trust his offish, clumsiness with something so precious as to risk ever asserting himself. This precious possession was hers— it was her— and she had to decide when and what she did with it. As long as, of course, she only ever did it with him.

There was no way he could go back to sleep. He sat up in the bed again, gently though, so as not to wake her. Sam waddled into the room and acknowledged Martin with a wag and a snort. He went to Christine's side and buried his muzzle under the bedding, sloppily licking her face.

"Sam you little git, all right I know you need to go out, bloody hell!"

She got out of the bed, her eyes still half shut.

"Bloody hell it's freezing! All right then, quickly you mutt!"

She was out of the room without so much as noticing the man she had been making love to only a few hours ago. He heard her distant voice from the downstairs kitchen door.

"Christ Sam hurry up, for God's sake boy haven't you ever seen a bit of snow before? Hurry up!"

The kitchen door slammed and he heard her angry footsteps clomping up the stairs. At the top of the staircase the footsteps stopped. And then she darted into the room.

"Hi! Look, shit this must look awful, when I'm half asleep I…so how are you, no I mean…"

She looked strangely smaller standing there in her nightie, her woolly jumper and her socks.

"Would you like me to …I mean I understand. I mean it's so obvious isn't it."

"What is?"

"Well, um, I mean, it's obvious that you've made a mistake, so..?"

"A mistake! What do you think of me Martin? The only mistake that I made was in being half asleep and being terribly rude to you for which I'm sorry. But I have certainly not made any other mistakes, and if you are referring to last night then I should have to be pretty bloody stupid to have mistaken that for anything else, shouldn't I ?"

"Well I—"

"Bollocks to you Daniels! I told you that I loved you and I still do, I really do! Do you have a problem with that?"

"No I—"

"Well then, would you please just accept it and let us get on with it because every time you doubt me, or assume that I'm going to change my mind, you make me feel like a brainless whore!"

"I'm sorry, I certainly—"

"I know you didn't Martin! Why do you think I love you?"

"I don't know, I honestly don't know."

She crawled onto the bed and held his face tenderly in her hands.

"You really don't do you? My God Martin do you have any idea how rare you are? Of course, you don't otherwise you wouldn't be that rare! Well, take it from me Martin, I'm a very lucky girl. And now I'm going to stop before your head expands and you become the very thing I hate."

She kissed him, a long soft kiss and then she whispered

"Would you like a cup of tea?"

"Yes, um, yes that would be very nice."

She shuffled back down the stairs whistling tunelessly to herself as she went.

The End...

Final Thoughts...

There is an ancient wisdom etched deep within our souls. Sometimes we see glimpses: I believe my near-death-experiences have enabled in me a certain foresight that makes it so that I can taste, smell, touch but not quite see clearly the teachings of eons ago. It tantalises me. If tasting death, twice, has taught me anything it is that time does not stand still while we get ready, whilst we prepare to do this or that: getting ready to do something simply equates to time lost that will never return. There is no such thing as failure: there is simply doing or not doing: that's it.

To that end I believe our ancestors had an easier time with time. They were only too aware of their own mortality, faced as they were with short life expectancy and the constant threat of death from danger or disease. I get the sense that theirs were lives lived to the fullest extent possible because knowing death gives you a clarity of thought and keenness of purpose...with the time you have left to live.

In many ways, death has become a taboo for us. Perhaps science and modern medicine creates in us a kind of buffer whereby the thought of certain death is given a caveat or two that enables us to off-set the inevitable, or somehow make it only really applicable to other poor souls. Not us: not yet...

I believe it's possible to have both a healthy relationship with death, your own 'crow-man' as it were; and to live a full, fearless life that is taking place in the here and now. And I mean right here right now. There is a theory I have, and it's actually quite complex and lengthy and I'll go into fully in a minute, about what lies behind the solution I'm going to suggest to you.

And I repeat this is a solution that will enable you to experience and to express yourself in the here and now forever and it applies to those with a brain injury and to those without. The solution is to practice T'ai Chi Qigong and meditation every day. The whole process as outlined in this book can take as little as 45 minutes a day to be profoundly effective. I said I'd explain my theory of why T'ai Chi can help humanity live fully and peacefully whilst staring death in the face; and whilst remaining robustly focused in the here and now…here we go.

We have certain terms, certain turns-of-phrase that give hints as to who we used to be. For millennia the human species changed really very little. Only in recent times has it been possible for people with strong minds and thoughts to be able to prevail without having equally strong bodies. The physical, visceral world of nature has been superseded by intellectual thought, design, technology and progress. But progress to what we recognise as modern-day society has wrought a terrible cost to the individual. Most of us have no idea who we are or where we have come from.

We have no real sense of identity or purpose because an entire physical language, that can still be seen clearly in nature, has become lost. As an example, going back to certain turns-of-phrase, when someone talks about 'their position on something' we know that they are referring to a way of thinking. However, this understanding is very, very recent. For most of humanity's experience and understanding, for eons and eons, the 'position' you took would refer to something physical. Attack or defence in swordsmanship. Heals down shoulders back when riding and so on.

I believe being in touch with the physical, visceral world can release in us our ancient, instinctual natures that attaches us, anchors us to the great unknown Power that is at the route of all existence; we need therefore to open the metaphysical door via engagement of the physical and spiritual: T'ai chi practice does this.

If God, or a Higher Power is almighty, then he/she/it IS ALMIGHTY; if God is EVERYWHERE then he/she/it is EVERYWHERE. I do not believe the creator of the universe to be choosy about HOW we get in touch. We already are in touch! God is everywhere, always. Like the sun, he/she/it always shines, it's just that we often live life in our own shadows.

If my near-death-experiences have taught me anything it is this: there is no narrative, linear existence. Everything that is, is. Right now. I did not expect to see the Crow-man. The Crow-man and I had/have no point of reference. It's literally nothing that I have ever experienced in any way shape or form before or after, and yet there he was: real and alive, visceral and physical. Right next to me. Moment by moment, breath by breath…

Many of us have had brushes with organised religion. In many ways I think Martin's rejection of the Priest in the 'Soulscape', as violent as it was, mirrored my own confusion and sense of spiritual desperation as a younger man. The truth for me now though is that God, or the Creator is simplicity itself. There is no linear narrative, no beginning, middle or end.

There is no right or wrong. And there is nowhere to get. You're already there. You and I are a part of a whole that is greater than comprehension and greater than contemplation: and yet we can, if we let go enough, savour the beautiful essence of all that is, in this moment, and the next and the next. Movement by movement, breath by breath, moment by moment…

I'm struggling. And when I struggle, I turn to poetry. This one was written for my dear Uncle Johnnie upon the loss of his beloved life-partner Maarten Peutz.

Eternal

Written in the darkness,
Hallowed by the light of love,
You stand on the lapping shore,
Waves frothing at your toes.
Love is all around us
And is bathing in your silent breath.
Love is all around us
And it radiates.
It radiates.
Written in the moonshine,
Lingering long on grassy banks,
Living in the thick-light
Of a rainy day in May.
Love is all around us,
And is bathing in your eyes that shine.
Love is all around us,
And it radiates,
It radiates.
Mystifying feelings,
Longing inside beings.
Written in the sand-dunes,
Is an ancient knowledge deep.
You are the dream, my alchemy
You are the light that shines.

Love is all around me,
And I'm bathing in your golden light,
Love is all around me
And it radiates,
It radiates.
You're no longer here.
No longer a part of here.
But written in the sun,
Blown on the mistral wind,
You rise.
Love is all around me,
And it radiates.
It radiates.
Love is all around me.
And it radiates.
It radiates.

About the Author

Jason Riddington is a professional actor and teacher. He began his screen career playing Hareton Earnshaw in Peter Kosminsky's *Wuthering Heights* opposite Juliette Binoche and Ralph Fiennes. Major television performances followed including Dr Rob Khalefa in the BAFTA award winning series 13 of *Casualty*; South-African Ashley Davies in *Inspector Morse* opposite John Thaw and Kevin Whately; further TV appearances include *Eastenders, A Touch of Frost, Berlin breaks, Bugs, Second Thoughts, The Bill, Family Affairs, Highlander* and most recently, *Luther* with Idris Elba and *Birds of a Feather* opposite Pauline Quirke, Lesley Joseph and Linda Robson. Further film credits include Edmund in Brian Blessed's *King Lear*, Paul in *Where There's Smoke*, and The Man in Jason Hreno's *Wondering Eyes*.

A classically trained actor at LAMDA, London, many major stage roles include the title roles in *Hamlet*, (the rehearsal process and performances being featured in Tony Lee's BBC2 documentary *Playing the Dane*) and *MacBeth*; Geoffrey in *The Lion in Winter* opposite Brian Blessed, Demetrius in *A Midsummer Night's Dream*, Heathcliff in *Wuthering Heights*, and his first professional role as Peachum in *The Beggar's Opera* with Nick Moran; and very recently with Nick Moran again (20 years later!) in Bill Kenwright's West End hit *12 Angry Men*, playing a range of parts with, among the incredible cast, Martin Shaw, Jeff Fahey and Robert Vaughn - finishing the run in the leading role Juror 8. Jason wrote the original story for the award-winning short film *Motherland*, currently on Amazon Prime, in which he plays co-lead, opposite the captivatingly talented Sope Dirisu.

An experienced and highly qualified teacher of acting, until his SAH Jason combined performing with teaching at some of London's top drama schools, he was also Head of Drama at prestigious Bedford Modern School 2003-2011. He has been a teacher and practitioner of T'ai Chi Qigong for 30 years.

He lives with his wife Faye in the beautiful Buckinghamshire countryside. They currently have four horses and two dogs! He has three grown up children Emily, Mikey and Phoebe and grand-daughter Leila.

On June 29th 2021 he suffered a massive subarachnoid haemorrhage and was admitted to John Radcliffe Hospital for emergency brain surgery. He suffered further life-threatening complications with a seizure on the 10th July 2021. After a total of four bouts of brain surgery he was discharged from hospital on July 29th 2021. He now focuses upon writing, his Personal Training business, T'ai Chi practice and teaching, and recovering from his brain injury.

About the Illustrator

Gregor Copeland is an artist and professional actor from Milton Keynes, now based in North London. He graduated from The Royal Birmingham Conservatoire in 2021 with a BA in Acting and has worked on numerous short films, tv adverts and stage productions in the year since graduating. Gregor began developing his artistic style and commissioning work during the first lockdown. His art is inspired by personal stories, world events and music. He uses symbolism and motifs to create simple but thought-provoking drawings and collages. Jason taught Gregor at school which was one of the reasons he pursued a career in acting.

Reading Jason's story and being moved and inspired by his words, Gregor was delighted to accept the offer to illustrate this book. Gregor has combined the mediums of drawings and collage for this project. His process has involved using pictures from Jason's journey and other photography to create the necessary shapes and lines of the illustrations. He has used the tracings from these photographs and combined them with his own drawings inspired by the story. He aimed to make illustrations that would be a catalyst for thought and imagination for the readers and hopes everyone will finish the book feeling as inspired as he was.

My Grateful Thanks

June 2022,

Without my wife Faye's quick-fired actions in calling the emergency services and administering CPR on that fateful day, June 29th 2021, I would be dead. Her continued monitoring of my mental and physical well-being and her unconditional love and support make my life not merely possible and tolerable but truly a gift that I appreciate so much every day. I owe her everything. And I'm the luckiest guy around to have such a 'wonder-woman' for a wife. Thank you Faye!

Thanks too to my incredible mum Jackie Smith-Autard and to my brother Ryan. What a terrible thing to have to witness for them both, their love and support has been amazing. And in many ways it's because of my mum's stellar encouragement (and eagle-eyed typo spotting, of which there was plenty let me assure you!) that you're reading this book in the first place! Thanks mum!

Thank you too to Faye's parents Roger and Jean, we stayed with them when I first left hospital and they have helped so much in the day-to-day of my recovery. Their love and support has been awesome. Thank you Roger and Jean!

Thanks so much to my incredible kids Emily, Mikey and Phoebe who have shown such amazing strength and faith throughout this traumatic time. Their continued love and support is extraordinary: they so nearly lost their dad. What a terrible thing that must have been for them. Thank you kids for showing me so much love and encouragement! And thanks to

Claire for taking the helm with Phoebe's education and being so supportive whilst I attempt to recover. Thank you!

Thanks too, to our amazing illustrator Gregor. I had the pleasure of teaching Gregor drama at Bedford Modern School and have kept in touch since he graduated from Birmingham Conservatoire. I find his artwork to be an absolute synthesis of what I try to say in preceding chapters, and truly, as a brain injury survivor I find his work so captivating because he somehow manages to encompass the whole issue pictorially! An amazing artist! Thank you Gregor.

Thanks to my dear old friend Brian Blessed, whose steadfast encouragement is the reason this books exists. He remains the truest example of life lived to the full, with bravery and integrity and I thank him for his unwavering support during the most challenging of times. Thank you Brian.

And finally thanks to all of the surgeons and staff at the Neurosurgical wards, Intensive Care wards and the Eye Hospital of John Radcliffe Hospital Oxford. You guys saved my life, repeatedly and your continued, incredible, relentless care, skill and support is unbelievable. Thank you!

If you have you been affected by brain injury, or any of the issues raised in this book; or, if you would like to know more about T'ai Chi Qigong you can contact the author directly at jason@mindfulbodyfit.co.uk